The Law of Medical Malpractice in Texas

The Law of Medical Malpractice in Texas

A Primer for the Medical Community

by Alan K. Laufman

Foreword by Charles S. Petty, M.D.

Illustrations by Susan Ingram
and Sally Blakemore-Turner

University of Texas Press, Austin & London

Library of Congress Cataloging in Publication Data

Laufman, Alan K
The law of medical malpractice in Texas.

Bibliography: p.
1. Physicians—Texas—Malpractice. 2. Medical personnel—Texas—Malpractice. I. Title. [DNLM: 1. Malpractice. 2. Physician-patient relation. W44 L373L]
KF1526.3.L38 346'.764'033 77-420
ISBN 0-292-74620-2

Set in Primer by G & S Typesetters, Inc.

Printed in the United States of America

Contents

Foreword xi

Acknowledgments xvii

1. The Patient-Physician Relationship 3

1.00 Creation of the Patient-Physician Relationship 3

Childs v. *Weis* 4
Notes 7
1. Express and implied contracts 7
2. Telephone conversations 7

1.01 Abandonment 9

Lee v. *Dewbre* 10
Notes 12
1. Plaintiff's burden of proof 12
2. Reasonable notice 12
3. Unilateral severance 12
4. Other forms of abandonment 12

1.02 Contract to Cure 14

Notes 15
1. Contract liability 15
2. Reassurances vs. warranties 15

II. NEGLIGENCE 17

2.00 General Theory of Negligence 17

2.01 Creation of Duty 18

2.02 Standard of Care 19

A. Diagnosis and Treatment 20
Henderson v. *Mason* 20
Traylor v. *Goulding* 22
Notes 24
1. Requirement for expert testimony 24
2. The same school rule 24
3. The locality rule 26
4. Error of judgment 27
5. The presumption in favor of the physician and *res ipsa loquitur* 28

B. Failure to Recommend Further Care 30
Martisek v. *Ainsworth* 30
Notes 32
1. Negligence in the premature release of a patient 32

C. Failure to Consult a Specialist 33
King v. *Flamm* 33
Notes 36
1. References on duty to consult 36

D. The Texas "Good Samaritan" Law 37
Notes 38
1. Purpose and effect of "Good Samaritan" statutes 38
2. Incidence of cases 38

2.03 Proximate Cause 39

Bender v. *Dingwerth* 40
Levermann v. *Cartall* 43

Notes 46
1. The requirement for proximate cause 46
2. The "reasonable probability" test 46
3. Requirement for expert testimony 47
4. Misdiagnosis and delay of treatment 48

III. VICARIOUS LIABILITY 51

3.00 Introduction 51

3.01 Liability for Acts of Hospital Personnel 53

A. Nurses 53
McKinney v. *Tromly* 53
Notes 55
1. "Captain of the ship" doctrine 55 (and 109)
2. Liability for negligent sponge count 55
3. Routine nursing care 55
4. Nurse's liability 56

B. Interns and Residents 57
McConnell v. *Williams* 57
Notes 59
1. Vicarious liability in nonsurgical setting 59
2. Negligence committed in presence of physician 59
3. Duty to discover intern or resident negligence 60
4. Personal liability of intern and resident 60
5. Hospital liability 60

3.02 Liability for Negligence of Office Employees 61

Rosenblum v. *Bloom* 61
Notes 62
1. The doctrine of *respondeat superior* 62
2. Injections 62
3. Delegation of duties 62

3.03 Liability for Acts of Another Physician 63

Notes 63
1. Responsibility for negligence of substitute 63
2. Responsibility for negligence of specialist 63
3. Partnership liability 64

IV. THE REQUIREMENT FOR PATIENT CONSENT 65

4.00 The Cause of Action: Battery or Informed Consent? 65

Moss v. *Rishworth* 67
Luna v. *Nering* 69
Notes 71
1. General consent forms 71
2. Special consent forms 71
3. Consent by a minor 72
4. Marriage and the capacity to consent 75
5. Consent by a spouse 75
6. Implied consent during medical emergency 75
7. Extension of authorized surgery 76
8. The surgeon's assistant 77

4.01 The Doctrine of Informed Consent 78

A. The Patient's Right to Self-Determination 78
Notes 79
1. History of informed consent 79

B. General Standard for the Duty to Disclose 81
Ross v. *Sher* 82
Notes 84
1. The majority rule 84
2. Application of the majority rule 84
3. The minority rule 85
4. Insufficiency of technical language 86

5. Information due without request; waiver 87
6. Capacity to grant informed consent 88

C. Scope of the Disclosure Requirement 89
Notes 90
1. General topics for disclosure 90
2. The range of risks to disclose 91
3. Information that need not be disclosed 92
4. Disclosure of alternatives 94
5. New or unusual treatment 94
6. Drug side effects 95
7. Physician objections to informed consent 95

D. Proximate Cause 97
Notes 98
1. An example of the proximate cause hurdle 98

4.02 Exceptions to the Requirement for Informed Consent 99

A. The Apprehensive Patient 99
Notes 101
1. Guidelines for exercising the therapeutic privilege 101
2. Liability for deception 102
3. The patient's right to decline treatment 102
4. Disclosure to the patient's family 102

B. Medical Emergency 104
Notes 105
1. Emergency treatment without consent 105

4.03 General Guidelines 106

Postscript to Section 3.01 109

Note on Legal Citations 113

Bibliography 115

Foreword

Fear of the unknown may be irrational but it afflicts many. The unknown embraces all those areas of life with which the individual is not familiar and in the presence of which one is uncomfortable. The physician is not immune to fear of the unknown, despite courses in and experience with psychology and psychiatry. In a very real sense, perhaps there is a larger unknown area for physicians than for others by virtue of their greater awareness of the complexities of life, and because of the narrowly defined specialty of medicine. The latter trait perhaps leads to intense exploration of a very narrow strip of life, leaving all other areas in the unknown sector. To the physician, the law and its many ramifications certainly represent the very depth of the unknown and may bring about the very apogee of fear—fear of the unknown, irrational fear.

One of the reasonable goals of the education of medical students should be to illuminate those very areas with which the physician will have contact. This, in turn, should eliminate areas of unknown and, therefore, decrease the hazard of allowing fear of the unknown to develop. There can be no question that today many facets of the law impinge as never before upon the practice of medicine. Not just that the two professions rub against each other, but rather that law and medicine have shown a need for each other and depend upon an understanding of each other.

For reasons unclear, most medical schools have failed to provide medical students with even a glimpse of that large area termed Law, which remains unknown and, therefore, a source of fear to the student. Fear of the unknown. Real fear that affects physicians and causes them to react by claiming they "should not be sued," that "the extent of damages to the physician should be limited"; in essence, that the doctor is above the law!

But the law needs the physician. Medical testimony is necessary in a very high percentage of cases tried in the courts. Medical evaluation of the claimant is necessary in most workmen's compensation cases. Examination of the rape or murder victim is becoming the standard. Medical skills are essential to the legal interpretation in many different types of cases at law. But, because of disinterest, apathy, a narrow definition of medicine, and fear, most medical students are really not aware of this.

In Texas, whether by design or chance, by statute law the applicant for licensure in medicine must be examined in medical jurisprudence. This subject might be termed "legal medicine" or perhaps "the parallel streams of law and medicine." At the University of Texas Southwestern Medical School at Dallas, a 26-hour course in medical jurisprudence is offered all fourth-year students. This course is designed to eliminate the area of law as an unknown area to the medical student and thereby to decrease the fear of the unknown.

Perhaps some of the great reactions to the so-called malpractice crisis derive from fear of the unknown by physicians. Perhaps this has prompted some of the outcry by physicians that they have been selected as targets by attorneys; that medicine is being discriminated against; that the law, long protective to physicians, is now aimed at destroying the individual practioner of medicine.

I do not believe this. I do believe that litigation is much more popular today than it was ten, twenty, or thirty years ago and that this includes, of course, suits against physicians. I do believe that physicians as a class represent inviting targets in some instances because of prominence and wealth and in other situations because of the charisma of modern medicine. I do believe that it is past time for physicians to realize that they, too, are bound by laws enacted by reasonable people for the conduct and regulation of society. It is past time for physicians to realize that, if their profession fails to regulate its own conduct, legal constraints to accomplish this will soon be established. Many broad concepts are involved, including continuing medical education, accreditation of medical laboratory facilities, delineation of the doctrine of informed consent by statute as a parameter of medical practice, and many other areas vital to the practice of medicine and dear to the heart of the physician.

Alan Laufman has written a monograph that should be fascinating to the medical students and physicians of Texas. He has written about Texas law as it affects the practice of medicine in Texas. His point of view as a young attorney, and now a second-year student of medicine, is especially fresh, revealing, and palatable to the student of medicine and the practitioner of medicine. His monograph is unique. All who read it must benefit, for he reduces the area of the unknown, and the fear of the unknown.

Perhaps some overviews might be offered. A few broad strokes on the canvas might make Mr. Laufman's detailed painting more meaningful.

1. In virtually all cases of medical negligence (medical malpractice) a physician serving as an expert witness is necessary to establish the *standard* of medical practice against which the medical defendant will be judged. Physicians, then, determine how their colleagues will be appraised in the courtroom. When a well qualified physician avoids the role of expert witness because of fear of the unknown, a much less well qualified physician may step forward, and more "malpractice friction" may result with deterioration of justice. How fortunate it is to have physicians, rather than non-medically trained persons, establish the standard. Attorneys have long lamented the so-called conspiracy of silence, when qualified physicians cannot be found to testify in court on the side of the plaintiff in medical negligence cases. This evasive action is probably

prompted by fear. But there are other little-used legal methods at hand to ensure adequate medical testimony or to avoid altogether the need for the medical expert witness. Such legal remedies may be employed to the gradual elimination of physicians themselves in providing the standard against which colleagues will be measured.

2. With the rise of paramedical personnel and the increasing utilization of such by physicians in the office, at the hospital, in the medical laboratory, and in the clinic, it is most important that practicing physicians understand thoroughly when they are legally obligated by the actions of paramedical personnel and how much follow-through they must apply. Should they be concerned with qualifications and hiring practices and can they be legally required to help in the continuing education and supervision of these non-physicians who may be indispensable in providing adequate health care? Is the surgeon really the "captain of the ship" in the operating room? If so, is he or she really responsible for the actions of the practitioner of anesthesiology before, during, and after the surgery?

3. Informed consent is a much-debated concept, or doctrine. Overwhelm patients with details concerning the therapeutic options, variables, and hazards and they will be staggered with decisions with which they may be unable to cope. Gloss over these and the physician may well have denied the patient his or her legal ("civil?") rights. And, as if these dilemmas are not enough, let physicians be active in clinical experimental work. How then do they approach their human "guinea pigs"?

All physicians in all states of the Union must conduct themselves according to the statutes regulating the practice of medicine. These laws tend to be very broadly worded, and great latitude is given the "Board," composed of practitioners of medicine. But state regulation of many, if not most, areas that impinge upon the public is becoming more clearly defined, carefully detailed, and specifically delineated. There does not seem to be any overriding reason for medicine to be overlooked in this trend. But undue delay

The Law of Medical Malpractice in Texas

Chapter I

The Patient-Physician Relationship

1.00 CREATION OF THE PATIENT-PHYSICIAN RELATIONSHIP

A physician is under no legal obligation to render services to a patient until a patient-physician relationship has been established. The relationship is wholly voluntary—it arises by an agreement between the patient and physician which may be either express or implied (*Childs* v. *Weis*, 440 S.W. 2d 104, 107 [Tex. Civ. App.—Dallas 1969]).

Childs v. *Weis*, 440 S.W.2d 104 (Tex. Civ. App.—Dallas 1969)

Statement of Facts

1. On November 27, 1966, Mrs. P, a resident of Garland, Texas, was visiting in Lone Oak, Texas. At the time, she was approximately seven months pregnant. Late that night she began to experience labor pains and went to the Greenville Surgical Hospital Emergency Room. She was examined there by Nurse N.

2. According to Mrs. P, Nurse N stated that she would call the doctor. She said the nurse returned and stated "that the doctor said that I would have to go to my doctor in Dallas. I stated to N that I'm not going to make it to Dallas. N replied that yes, I would make it. She stated that I was just starting into labor and that I would make it. . . . About an hour after leaving the Greenville Hospital Authority, I had the baby while in a car on the way to medical facilities in Sulphur Springs. The baby lived about 12 hours."

3. Dr. D stated that he had never examined or treated Mrs. P and in fact had never seen or spoken to either her or her husband at any time in his life. He further stated that he had never at any time agreed or consented to the examination or treatment of either Mrs. P or her husband. He said that on a day in November 1966 he received a telephone call from a nurse in the emergency room at the Greenville Surgical Hospital; that the nurse told him there was a girl in the emergency room having a "bloody show" and some "labor pains." He said the nurse advised him that this woman had been visiting in Lone Oak, and that her OB doctor lived in Garland, Texas, and that she also resided in Garland. The doctor went on to testify, "I told the nurse over the telephone to have the girl call her doctor in Garland and see what he wanted her to do. I knew noth-

ing more about this incident until I was served with the citation and a copy of the petition in this lawsuit."

4. The trial court dismissed the case and entered a verdict for Dr. D. The case was then appealed to the Court of Appeals in Dallas.

Issue before the Court

Did the nurse's telephone call to Dr. D create a patient-physician relationship between Mrs. P and the doctor—and thereby impose certain duties on Dr. D?

Decision of the Court

The court held that the nurse's telephone call to Dr. D did not create a patient-physician relationship. Therefore, a verdict was rendered in favor of the physician.

> The *sine qua non* of [Mrs. P's] cause of action against Dr. D is the existence of a duty on the part of Dr. D to do those things that an ordinarily prudent physician would do . . . in the proper care and treatment of his patient. The existence of the duty must flow from the relationship of patient-physician. . . . Since it is unquestionably the law that the relationship of physician and patient is dependent upon contract, either express or implied, a physician is not to be held liable for arbitrarily refusing to respond to a call of a person urgently in need of medical or surgical assistance provided that the relation of physician and patient does not exist at the time the call is made or at the time the person presents himself for treatment. . . .
>
> Applying these principles of law to the factual situation here presented we find an entire absence of evidence of a contract, either express or implied, which would create the relationship of patient and physician as between Dr. D and Mrs. P. Dr. D, under these cir-

cumstances, was under no duty whatsoever to examine or treat Mrs. P. When advised by telephone that the lady was in the emergency room he did what seems to be a reasonable thing and inquired as to the identity of her doctor who had been treating her. Upon being told that the doctor was in Garland he stated that the patient should call the doctor and find out what should be done. This action on the part of Dr. D seems to be not only reasonable but within the bounds of professional ethics.

We cannot agree with [plaintiff] that Dr. D's statement to the nurse over the telephone amounted to an acceptance of the case. . . . Rather than give instructions which could be construed to be in the nature of treatment, Dr. D told the nurse to have the woman call her physician in Garland and secure instructions from him. (440 S.W.2d at 106–107)

Notes

1. Express and implied contracts

As seen in *Childs*, a physician may not be held liable for failing to treat a patient unless a patient-physician relationship existed between the parties. The question of whether conduct in a given case gave rise to the requisite relation is answered by determining if an express or implied contract was made between the parties.

In the uncommon case where the parties reached an explicit agreement (oral or written) concerning the patient's medical care, the courts will find that an "express contract" was made. In the absence of an explicit agreement, the courts ostensibly look for an "implied contract" between the patient and physician. Unfortunately, there is no clear standard for this evaluation. But, generally speaking, if the physician offers any form of medical assistance, be it advice or treatment, the courts are likely to conclude that a patient physician relationship was established and hence the physician had a duty to follow through on the patient's case. (See "The Care Required of Medical Practitioners," 12 *Vand. L. Rev.* 549, 553–556 [1959]; Holder, *Medical Malpractice Law*, 1–6 [1975].)

2. Telephone conversations

In several instances, telephone conversations have been found sufficient to establish the patient-physician relationship and subject the physician to liability for failing to attend a patient. (See "Creation of the Patient-Physician Relationship," 230 *JAMA* No. 2, 278, Oct. 14, 1974.) Consequently, the following advice has been offered:

> [I]f a physician is called by a stranger who relates symptoms and the physician does not wish to accept the person as a patient, he would be well advised to limit his advice to telling the person to go to a hospital emergency room or to seek medical assistance else-

where. If the patient is one who is or has been under the care of the physician, however, the physician is probably obligated to give advice, although if a duly careful physician would conclude that no emergency exists, the patient may, of course, be told to come to the office at an appropriate time. (230 *JAMA* No. 2 at 278)

1.01 ABANDONMENT

Abandonment of a patient by a doctor constitutes a legal wrong which can give rise to a claim for malpractice. Abandonment generally means the unilateral severance of the professional relationship between doctor and patient, in the absence of

(1) reasonable notice, *or*

(2) the provision of substitute medical care—

at a time when continuing medical attention is still needed.

Lee v. *Dewbre*, 362 S.W.2d 900, 902 (Tex. Civ. App.—Amarillo 1962)

Statement of Facts

1. On July 8, 1960, Mrs. P was admitted to the hospital by Dr. D. At that time, she was seven months pregnant. Dr. D had been her physician throughout the pregnancy.

2. Mrs. P's baby was born the next day (July 9). Immediately after the birth, extensive internal bleeding became evident and Mrs. P went into shock. Dr. E was called to assist Dr. D and together the two doctors repaired a laceration to the oviduct. In the hours following surgery the patient's condition began to improve. Dr. D remained with his patient until some time after midnight.

3. Dr. D saw his patient again the following morning (July 10). Later that day, he moved to another town and he did not see her again. Beginning that day, Dr. E assumed responsibility for the treatment of Mrs. P. Two days later she was transferred to another hospital and underwent a hysterectomy.

4. Mrs. P's family brought suit against Dr. D under the doctrine of abandonment. At the trial, there was a dispute in the evidence as to whether Dr. D had ever notified Mrs. P's family that he was withdrawing from the case.

5. The trial court held that Dr. D was liable for abandonment and the case was appealed to the Court of Appeals in Amarillo.

Issue before the Court

Did Dr. D's conduct toward Mrs. P constitute abandonment?

Decision of the Court

The court found that Dr. D, before withdrawing from Mrs.

P's case, adequately arranged substitute medical care. The plaintiff, Mrs. P, therefore failed to prove her allegation of abandonment.

> It will be noted that . . . there is actionable abandonment only in the absence of reasonable notice or of providing an adequate medical attendant. One of these two elements is the very crux of abandonment. In the instant case, there is no evidence that Mrs. P was ever without adequate medical attention. . . . In view of the undisputed evidence that Mrs. P did receive competent medical care until being released [from the hospital], we cannot say [plaintiffs] sustained their burden of proof of actionable abandonment on the part of Dr. D. (362 S.W.2d at 903)

Notes

1. Plaintiff's burden of proof

Lee v. *Dewbre* teaches that a plaintiff can recover on a theory of abandonment only if he proves:

(1) the existence of a patient-physician relationship,
(2) unilateral severance by the physician without reasonable notice *or* provision of alternative medical care,
(3) a necessity for continuing medical attention,
(4) causal connection between the severance of the relationship and the patient's injuries (proximate cause), and
(5) resulting damages.

2. Reasonable notice

The "reasonable notice" condition cited in Note 1 is satisfied when the patient is given ample opportunity to procure alternative medical attention if he so desires (*Lee* v. *Dewbre*, 362 S.W.2d 900, 903 [Tex. Civ. App.—Amarillo 1962]).

3. Unilateral severance

Abandonment can occur only if the physician *unilaterally* severs the patient-physician relationship. Thus, abandonment is not present if the relationship is terminated by mutual consent or the dismissal of the physician. (See Perdue, *The Law of Texas Medical Malpractice*, sec. 2.05 at 40 [1975].) For example, when a patient leaves the hospital against the doctor's wishes, the doctor cannot be held liable for failing to treat the patient further (*Miles* v. *Harris*, 194 S.W. 839, 844 [Tex. Civ. App.—Fort Worth 1917]).

4. Other forms of abandonment

The traditional doctrine of abandonment, as described in

the notes above, relates to the situation where a doctor improperly withdraws from a case. In recent years the term "abandonment" has also been used to describe a number of other situations: failure to see a hospitalized patient for several days (*Levy* v. *Kirk*, 187 So.2d 401, Fla. 1966); refusal to give a nurse instructions for a hospitalized patient (*Johnson* v. *Vaughn*, 370 S.W.2d 591, Ky. 1963); failure to attend a patient with recognizable symptoms of an impending miscarriage (*Michigan* v. *Sheehan*, 51 A2d 632, N.H. 1947); failure to attend a pregnant patient at time of delivery (*Norton* v. *Hamilton*, 89 S.E.2d 809, Ga. 1955); and failure to provide adequate coverage while temporarily out of town (*Livingston* v. *Portland General Hospital Assoc.*, 357 P.2d 543, Ore. 1960). (See "Abandonment," parts I–IV, 225 *JAMA* No. 9, 1157, Aug. 27, 1973; No. 10, 1285, Sept. 3, 1973; No. 11, 1429, Sept. 10, 1973; No. 12, 1511, Sept. 17, 1973; also "Abandonment—the Malpractice 'Catch-All,'" 71 *Texas Monthly* No. 4, 118, April 1975; Holder, *Medical Malpractice Law*, 376–393 [1975].)

1.02 CONTRACT TO CURE

In the absence of a special contract, a physician is not an insurer and does not warrant favorable results. All that the physician impliedly undertakes is that he or she possesses and will exercise the required degree of skill and care. Responsibility may, however, be enlarged by an express agreement which contractually binds the physician to obtain specific results (45 Tex. Jur. 2d, sec. 120).

Notes

1. Contract liability

To establish liability under contract theory, a plaintiff must prove that his physician made an express promise or warranty to achieve a particular result. If the plaintiff proves that such a contract was made and then violated, the physician will be liable for breach of contract, regardless of whether he was negligent in the treatment of his patient (*Weeks* v. *Heinrich*, 447 S.W.2d 688, 695 [Tex. Civ. App.—Corpus Christi 1969]).

2. Reassurances vs. warranties

Express promises should be distinguished from predictions, therapeutic reassurances, or expressions of hope which do not constitute legal warranties. (See Perdue, *The Law of Texas Medical Malpractice*, sec. 1.07 at 15 [1975].) However, there are many examples where a statement apparently intended to reassure the patient was construed by a court to amount to an agreement to effect a particular result. For example, such statements as "no danger at all in this operation," or the operation "will take care of all of your troubles," or the patient will be able to return to work in "approximately three weeks" have been construed to indicate that a contract was made between physician and patient. (See "Warranties or Guarantees of Results May Create Physician Liability," 72 *Texas Medicine* 89, May 1976; "Guarantee of Medical Results," 219 *JAMA* No. 3, 431, Jan. 17, 1972.)

In *Levine* v. *Carrell*, 68 S.W.2d 259 (Tex. Civ. App.—El Paso 1934), the plaintiff sought medical advice because she was unable to lift her right arm above her head. She was a typist by trade and except for this limitation the arm was functional in all respects. At the trial the plaintiff testified that, before she agreed to an operation, the doctor said "my right arm would be like my left arm when he got through with it." Despite the assurances, the operation resulted in permanent impairment of the woman's arm and she had to give up her job as a typist. The appellate court reversed the lower court's decision for the physician and stated:

> This evidence, in our opinion, clearly raised an issue as to an express agreement on the part of Dr. D that the operation would improve the condition of [plaintiff's] arm. . . . (68 S.W.2d at 262)

Chapter II

Negligence

2.00 GENERAL THEORY OF NEGLIGENCE

To obtain a judgment against a physician for malpractice, the patient (plaintiff) must prove that:

(1) the physician owed a duty to the patient (creation of patient-physician relationship—sec. 2.01),
(2) the physician was derelict in that duty (negligent breach of the legal standard of care—sec. 2.02),
(3) such dereliction was a direct cause of the patient's injury (proximate cause—sec. 2.03), and
(4) damages to the patient resulted from the physician's negligent acts.

2.01 CREATION OF DUTY

The legal duty of a physician to care for a patient arises when a patient-physician relationship is created (*Childs v. Weis*, 440 S.W.2d 104, 107 [Tex. Civ. App.—Dallas 1969]). (See Chapter I, sec. 1.00, Creation of the Patient-Physician Relationship.)

2.02 STANDARD OF CARE

A defendant-physician's conduct is measured against a community standard of care: a physician has a duty to use the degree of care, skill, and diligence which other physicians in the community (or a similar community) would exercise under similar circumstances (*Bowles* v. *Bourdon*, 148 Tex. 1, 219 S.W.2d 779, 782 [1949]).

A. Diagnosis and Treatment

Henderson v. *Mason*, 386 S.W.2d 879 (Tex. Civ. App.—El Paso 1964)

Statement of Facts

1. On Saturday night, February 11, 1961, while Mr. P was working on a job in Andrews, Texas, his right eye was injured by a piece of steel. He was taken to the Medical Center Hospital in Odessa, Texas, for emergency treatment.

2. Dr. D, an internist, was on duty in the emergency ward and saw Mr. P. Dr. D examined the injured eye with a pocket flashlight and administered some antibiotic drops. He advised his patient to see an eye specialist if he had any further problems.

3. Later that same evening, Mr. P's eye began bothering him, and his wife tried unsuccessfully to contact an ophthalmologist. However, on Sunday morning, Mr. P did see a specialist, Dr. E, who examined and X-rayed the injured eye. On Monday morning, Dr. E performed an operation to remove a small piece of steel from Mr. P's eye.

4. By April 1962, the patient had no vision in his injured eye. Subsequently, he brought a suit against Dr. D for negligence in diagnosis and treatment. The claim specifically alleged that Dr. D's failure to examine the eye with an ophthalmoscope and his failure to X-ray the eye constituted actionable negligence.

5. The trial court rendered a verdict for the defendant and the case was then appealed to the Court of Appeals in El Paso.

Issue before the Court

Did Dr. D's conduct in examining his patient violate the legal standard of care for internists?

Decision of the Court

The court found that Dr. D's examination of Mr. P met the standard of care required by law and therefore rendered a verdict for the defendant:

> The law presumes that the physician has done his work properly, and he is not considered by the law to be a guarantor or insurer. His obligation is to use his best judgment, both in diagnosis and treatment, and the plaintiff can recover only when it can be affirmatively shown—and this is the burden of the plaintiff—that the diagnosis or treatment was not an error in judgment, but a matter of negligence, and that such negligence was the proximate cause of the damages claimed by plaintiff. . . .
>
> [Where] the lawsuit or the issues deal with . . . the propriety of particular conduct of the physician . . . expert testimony favorable to plaintiff is indispensable, and without such, a plaintiff cannot recover. . . . It is clear from the evidence here that there is no expert testimony that defendant was negligent in any way in his diagnosis and treatment of the injury. With regard to the use of the ophthalmoscope, the defendant's testimony (that it would not be of any value in this particular type of case because it does not magnify sufficiently to be of any help) stands undisputed. Viewing the evidence as a whole we cannot find . . . that the defendant was guilty of any negligence, either in diagnosis or treatment. Even though [the plaintiff] accuses him of an error in judgment, the law does not hold the physician responsible for such unless it amounts to negligence, and there is none shown here by any testimony. (386 S.W.2d at 882)

Traylor v. *Goulding*, 497 S.W.2d 468 (Tex. Civ. App.—Houston 1973)

Statement of Facts

1. On March 8, 1966, Mrs. P saw her eighteen-month-old son, Dwayne Alan, swallow a chicken bone. The child gagged, coughed, and appeared to have difficulty in breathing. Mrs. P immediately gave first aid and then took the child to the emergency room of the Pasadena Bay Shore Hospital, where he was seen by a general practitioner, Dr. D. At that time the child's symptoms had disappeared. The doctor examined the child's throat and lungs and found no abnormality. He did not hospitalize the child.

2. On March 11, 1966, Mrs. P took the child back to the emergency room because he was coughing and running a high temperature. Dr. D was again on duty. He testified that he did not remember the child. Mrs. P testified that she told him about the chicken bone. Dr. D diagnosed bronchitis and prescribed penicillin. No X-rays were taken.

3. Several weeks later, Dwayne was readmitted to the hospital, suffering from fever and poor breathing. Bronchoscopy was performed by another doctor and a chicken bone was discovered and removed from the base of the right lung.

4. Mrs. P brought a suit against Dr. D for negligence. At the trial, the jury found that Dr. D's conduct did not constitute negligence. The case was then appealed to the Court of Appeals in Houston.

Issue before the Court

Did Dr. D's failure to perform bronchoscopy on his patient violate the standard of care demanded of a general practitioner and therefore constitute negligence?

Decision of the Court

The appellate court ruled that the jury's decision was adequately supported by the evidence. The court applied a standard of care appropriate for general practitioners:

> Neither does the evidence require a finding that Dr. D was negligent in failing to perform a bronchoscopy on the child. . . . There was evidence that general practitioners ordinarily do not perform that procedure. The doctor did not consider the procedure necessary. There was no evidence that a doctor should carry out that procedure under the circumstances known to Dr. D. (497 S.W.2d at 471)

Notes

1. Requirement for expert testimony

Recall that in *Henderson* v. *Mason* the court emphasized:

> [Where] the lawsuit or issues deal with . . . the propriety of particular conduct of the physician . . . expert testimony favorable to plaintiff is indispensable, and without such, a plaintiff cannot recover. . . . (386 S.W.2d at 882)

This language raises two important points. First, the courts do not allow juries to freely decide whether a physician's conduct in a given case was negligent. Rather, the standard of care governing the case is, in most instances, a "professional" standard—it is defined by the medical profession itself. This is done by means of an expert medical witness who testifies to the level of care which the plaintiff should have received. Second, it is the burden of the plaintiff to offer this expert testimony. The testimony must (1) establish the standard of care against which the defendant's conduct can be evaluated and (2) allow the inference to be made that the defendant violated the given standard of care and therefore is guilty of negligence. If the plaintiff should fail to satisfy these requirements, he will be subject to a preemptory dismissal of his case (directed verdict). (See Perdue, *The Law of Texas Medical Malpractice*, sec. 6.01 at 1.09 [1975]; "The Standard of Care," parts I–III, 225 *JAMA* No. 6, 671, Aug. 6, 1973; No. 7, 791, Aug. 13, 1973; No. 8, 1027, Aug. 20, 1973; also Holder, *Medical Malpractice Law*, 40–53 [1975].)

2. The same school rule

Technically, the legal standard for medical negligence states that the physician need only exercise that degree of skill as members of the "same school of practice" (*Porter* v. *Puryear*, 153 Tex. 82, 262 S.W.2d, 933, 935–936 [1953]). The evidentiary application of this rule generally obligates a plaintiff to prove his allegations of negligence with expert testimony from "a doctor of the same school of practice as the defendant" (*Bowles* v. *Bourdon*, 147 Tex. 608, 219 S.W.2d 779, 782 [1949]. The original purpose of the rule was to ensure that the performance of a general practitioner would be assessed by another general practitioner, that of an orthopedist by another orthopedist, and so on.

In recent years, the courts have considerably relaxed the same school rule. For example, in *Christian* v. *Jeter*, 445 S.W.2d 51 (Tex. Civ. App.—Waco 1969), plaintiff's expert witness was an orthopedic specialist and defendant was a general practitioner. The case concerned the general practitioner's treatment of a dislocated elbow. The specialist testified that X-rays should have been made of the patient's elbow after it was set. The general practitioner argued that testimony from an orthopedist was inadmissible under the same-school rule. In typical judicial fashion, the court "construed" the rule to allow the orthopedist to testify against the general practitioner:

> Under the facts of this case, they *are* of the "same school of medicine," notwithstanding [the fact that] the witness was an orthopedic specialist.
>
> Where the particular subject of inquiry is common to all fields of practice or where the subject of inquiry

> relates to the manner of use of electrical or mechanical appliances in common use in all fields of practice (as the record shows is true of X-rays in this case), the rule relating to admission of [expert] evidence in malpractice cases is qualified. (cite omitted). (445 S.W.2d at 54)

3. The locality rule

Another historical principle for evaluating medical negligence is the "locality rule," which states that a physician need only exercise that degree of skill possessed by physicians *in his or her community*. The evidentiary corollary of this rule requires the plaintiff to present expert testimony on the *local* standard of care, against which the defendant's conduct will be measured. As a practical consequence of this rule, a plaintiff is generally limited to recruiting expert witnesses from his home community.

However, like the same school rule, this doctrine has been considerably bent out of its original shape. In *Christian* v. *Jeter*, the case described in Note 2, the plaintiff sought to introduce expert testimony from a physician who practiced in Dallas. Because the defendant-physician practiced in Ennis, Texas, this testimony was objected to as a violation of the locality rule. The court overruled the objection:

> The fact that Dr. D was from Dallas did not preclude his testimony "concerning the medical standards of practice and treatment" in Ennis in this type of case. Sufficient familiarity with such standards was shown to make his evidence admissible. (445 S.W.2d at 53)

The court went on to discuss the original purpose of the locality rule and its modern-day interpretation in Texas:

> The present rule is summarized 8 A.L.R.2d 773: "In the days when there was little inter-community travel the courts required personal familiarity with the practice of physicians in the particular community where

> the plaintiff was treated as the basis for the expert's testimony." This was on the theory that a doctor in a small community did not have "the same opportunity or resources for keeping abreast of his profession." The reason for the rule has now disappeared with the advent of modern transportation and communication, with no lack of opportunity to keep abreast of methods and practices. The controlling factor in determining competency now is that the medical witness have "practical knowledge of what is usually and customarily done by other practitioners under circumstances similar to those which confronted the defendant charged with malpractice." (445 S.W.2d at 53–54)

While Texas courts continue to expand and qualify the old locality rule, courts in other states have expressly abandoned the doctrine. In its place they have adopted a rule whereby the required standard of care and skill is that of the average practitioner under the same or similar circumstances. With this approach, the locality of practice is merely a factor to be considered in determining whether a negligent act was committed. (See Perdue, *The Law of Texas Medical Malpractice*, sec. 2.04 at 35–37 [1975]; Holder, *Medical Malpractice Law*, 53 [1975].)

4. Error of judgment

In *Henderson* v. *Mason, infra*, the court recites the principle that "the plaintiff can recover only when it can be affirmatively shown . . . that the diagnosis or treatment was not an error in judgment but a matter of negligence" (386 S.W.2d at 882). The Texas origin of the "best judgment" rule is the first malpractice case to be reported in the state, *Graham* v. *Gautier*, 21 Tex. 111 (1858). The decision in that case stated:

> That is, after he has, with reasonable care and diligence, exercised ordinary skill, he is not responsible for a mistake of judgment, or for the result if he should happen to be mistaken. (21 Tex. at 120)

Unfortunately, courts often invoke the "mistake of judgment" principle without first analyzing the physician's performance. Properly applied, the doctrine requires an assessment of the "intermediate" steps leading to the physician's exercise of judgment. If the physician is found to have had a sound foundation for the medical decision reached and the decision itself does not clearly violate medical standards, the physician should be exonerated. (See Louisell and Williams, *Medical Malpractice*, vol. 1, sec. 804 at 204 [1970]; Perdue, *The Law of Texas Medical Malpractice*, sec. 2.02, 26–28 [1975].)

More specifically, it has been suggested that, when negligence in the physician's diagnosis is alleged, the mistake of judgment defense should be recognized only if one of the following factors was present:

(1) there is reasonable doubt as to the nature of the physical condition involved;
(2) there is a split of recognized medical authority as to the appropriate diagnostic procedure, one of which is followed; or
(3) the diagnosis is made after a conscientious effort by the physician to inform himself of the symptoms and physical state of the patient (23 *Vand. L. Rev.* 729, 749 [1970].

See "Misdiagnosis without Fault," parts I–II, 219 *JAMA* No. 7, 967, Feb. 14, 1972; No. 8, 1127, Feb. 21, 1972.

5. The presumption in favor of the physician and *res ipsa loquitur*

Some Texas cases analyze the standard of care issue in terms of a presumption in favor of the physician which must be overcome by the plaintiff. In *Thomas* v. *Beckering*, 391 S.W.2d 771 (Tex. Civ. App.—Tyler 1965), the court explains this principle:

> It is well settled that the law entertains in favor of a physician, or surgeon, the presumption that he has

> discharged his full duty. . . . to overcome such presumption the law exacts affirmative proof, both of breach of duty and that such breach resulted in injury. Negligence, in such cases, is never imputed from mere results, nor can any inference of negligence be indulged against a physician or surgeon from the results. (391 S.W.2d at 775)

Stinnett v. *Price*, 446 S.W.2d 893 (Tex. Civ. App.—Amarillo 1969), provides an example of an unfortunate "result" which alone could not support a finding of negligence. The plaintiff in that case suffered a stroke a few hours after the defendant-physician administered an angiogram. The plaintiff failed to offer any expert testimony to support his allegation that the doctor had been negligent in ordering or performing the angiogram. The plaintiff thus relied entirely on an inference of negligence from the mere occurrence of the stroke. The court cited the Texas rule that negligence may not be inferred from a bad result of treatment and dismissed the case (446 S.W.2d at 896).

Despite the pronouncements of cases like *Thomas* v. *Beckering* and *Stinnett* v. *Price*, Texas courts may in certain exceptional circumstances permit the plaintiff to rely on an inference of negligence rather than direct expert testimony. The doctrine invoked is known as *res ipsa loquitur* (the thing speaks for itself). Its applicability is circumscribed by several conditions. Most importantly, it is limited to cases involving an injury which would ordinarily not occur in the absence of negligence. The classic example is the case in which a sponge or other "foreign object" is left in a patient's body during surgery.

The application of the doctrine to medical malpractice cases in Texas remains controversial. (See Perdue, *The Law of Texas Medical Malpractice*, chap. 5, 89–100 [1975].)

B. Failure to Recommend Further Care

Martisek v. *Ainsworth*, 459 S.W.2d 679 (Tex. Civ. App.—Houston 1970)

Statement of Facts

1. In November 1962, Mr. P fell while working on a fire escape near the third-floor level of a hotel building. He sustained serious injuries and was taken to the hospital where he was examined by Dr. D, an orthopedist. Among the injuries diagnosed were a fracture of the left elbow and a fracture of the left heel bone. Casts were placed on the left arm and left leg. X-rays taken the next day revealed compression fractures of two vertebrae.

2. Mr. P was permitted to leave the hospital after two weeks. At the trial there was testimony that Dr. D (a) told Mr. P that his back was "all right" and prescribed no specific treatment for the back injuries, and (b) gave no instructions to Mr. P concerning limitations on activities due to the back condition.

3. In March 1963, Mr. P returned to his job, doing light work for two hours a day. The hours were increased until he was back at an eight-hour day by the first months of 1964. On January 22, 1965, he assisted a fellow employee in lifting a metal frame weighing seventy pounds and as a result suffered a herniated lumbar disk. This injury led to an operation and further disability.

4. The orthopedic surgeon who treated Mr. P after the 1965 incident testified that his patient "had a weak back and that it was taken past its limits, causing protrusion of disk material." The doctor also gave an opinion that the injuries to the ligaments sustained in the 1962 accident made the patient's back vulnerable to the injury which occurred in 1965. He further testified that a physician

who told a patient like Mr. P that his back was all right, and failed to give him "specific cautions" with respect to his back, fell below the standard of ordinary care of a physician practicing in the area.

5. The trial court found that the plaintiff's expert testimony on the standard of care was insufficient to prove that Dr. D had been negligent. The judge directed a verdict for the physician and the case was appealed to the Court of Appeals in Houston.

Issue before the Court

Was the evidence concerning Dr. D's failure to advise his patient of the back condition and to recommend further care sufficient to raise the issue of negligence for the jury?

Decision of the Court

The Court of Appeals reversed the trial court's decision and ordered a new trial.

The court reviewed the testimony given by the orthopedic surgeon and concluded:

> The testimony is sufficient to raise an issue for the jury as to whether or not Dr. D was negligent in failing to inform Mr. P of the injury to his back, its nature, and the resultant limitations on the use of his back. (459 S.W.2d at 680)

Notes

1. Negligence in the premature release of a patient

Martisek v. *Ainsworth* illustrates that a physician may violate the requisite standard of care if he or she fails to advise a patient of physical limitations resulting from an injury. In a similar vein, there are a few Texas cases alleging negligence in the premature release of a patient from a doctor's care. In *Kinion* v. *Hyde*, 471 S.W.2d 920 (Tex. Civ. App.—Amarillo 1971), an orthopedic surgeon treated the plaintiff's fractured wrist and released her several months later. At the time of her release she still complained of pain. Later it was determined that the bone had healed in an unsatisfactory position. A decision was rendered for the orthopedist because experts testified at the trial that further treatment was not warranted at the time of release. (Cf. *Conrey* v. *McGehee*, 473 S.W.2d 617 [Tev. Civ. App.—Houston 1971]. See also "Abandonment," part I, 225 *JAMA* No. 9, 1157 at 1158, Aug. 27, 1973.)

C. Failure to Consult a Specialist

King v. *Flamm*, 442 S.W.2d 679 (Tex. 1969)

Statement of Facts

1. Several weeks after some minor surgery, Mrs. P awoke with a pain in the left side of her chest. She called Dr. D, a general practitioner, and he advised her to take a Darvon capsule. When the pain continued the following day, she saw Dr. D's associate, Dr. E. She was X-rayed and Dr. E diagnosed her condition as pleurisy and gave her some medication. Over the next three days, Mrs. P continued to experience pain and Dr. E prescribed additional medication.

2. On November 11, 1966, Mrs. P coughed up "a tremendous clot of blood." She called Dr. D and advised him of her symptoms. He told her the blood was not coming from her lungs and that she had nothing to worry about. During the next several days, her pain continued and she coughed up blood occasionally.

3. On November 17, she had fever for the first time. She called Dr. D and he prescribed another antibiotic. On November 20, she awoke in extreme pain and with a relatively high temperature. She again called Dr. D and he had her admitted into the hospital. At that time, she told him that she was concerned about her condition and requested him to call in a specialist. Dr. D advised her that he had viewed the X-rays taken upon her admission to the hospital, that she had lobar pneumonia, and that he did not think it was necessary to call in a consultant for this condition.

4. The continued use of antibiotics brought Mrs. P's temperature to normal, and she was discharged from the hospital on December 5. She coughed up dark clots of blood three times during this period of hospitalization. Dr. D's

diagnosis as dictated on December 5 was "admitting diagnosis: Bronchopneumonia, right chest. Final: Pneumonia, right middle lobe. Pleurisy with effusion at both bases."

5. Mrs. P did very well for a few days at home, but on December 18 "suddenly had the terrible pains and the coughing of blood again." She called Dr. D who sent her more medication. Her temperature gradually diminished, and she was feeling "pretty good" by Christmas. She continued to cough up blood, however, one or more times each day. She was X-rayed again on December 30 and Dr. D advised that her lungs had cleared up considerably but not completely, and that she could return to her secretarial work after the holidays. She went back to work on January 2, 1967, and the following day began coughing up blood two or three times every hour.

6. Mrs. P was again admitted to the hospital on January 5. Dr. D's initial diagnosis at that time was "chest pain, cough with bloody sputum, cause undetermined." Mrs. P again requested that Dr. D call a specialist and he agreed to do so. The following day she was seen by Dr. F, who promptly diagnosed her condition as pulmonary embolism resulting from thrombophlebitis in the lower extremities and the pelvic area. Mrs. P was then placed on conservative treatment for pulmonary embolism.

7. In a pretrial deposition, the plaintiff's expert witness stated positively that "during one of these spells when she was in the hospital and having so much trouble . . . most general practitioners would have and should have called in a specialist."

8. In a pretrial hearing, the defendant, Dr. D, argued that Mrs. P had failed to submit sufficient evidence on the issue of negligence and therefore the case should be dismissed. The trial court dismissed the case and the plaintiff appealed to the Court of Appeals and then to the Supreme Court of Texas.

Issue before the Court

Was the pretrial evidence concerning Dr. D's failure to consult a specialist sufficient to establish negligence and warrant a full-scale trial?

Decision of the Court

The Supreme Court of Texas reversed the trial court decision and ordered a new trial.

In its decision, the court emphasized the testimony from Mrs. P's expert witness that "most general practitioners would have and should have called a specialist." The court concluded that the case would have to be formally tried and it would be up to the jury to determine whether Dr. D's failure to consult a specialist was actionable negligence.

The court made the following statement on the duty of a general practitioner to consult a specialist:

> The general practitioner is not required to consult with a specialist, however, on every conceivable complication that may arise in his practice. If he exercises the care and skill of other physicians similarly situated, he is not responsible for an error of judgment even though a specialist would not have made the same mistake. But there is a duty to seek consultation with, or refer the patient to, a specialist when he knows, or in the exercise of reasonable care should know, that the services of a specialist are indicated. Here, as in other cases of alleged medical malpractice, the defendant is to be judged on the basis of the standards and practices of his profession. If there is expert testimony fairly supporting the conclusion that a reasonably careful and prudent general practitioner would have sought consultation under the same or similar circumstances, the trier of fact is entitled to find that the defendant was negligent in failing to do so. (442 S.W.2d at 681)

Notes

1. References on duty to consult

The duty to consult is discussed in Holder, *Medical Malpractice Law*, 45–59 (1975); "Duty to Consult Orthopedic Specialist," 204 *JAMA* No. 7, 249, May 13, 1968; "Duty to Refer Patient to Medical Specialist," 204 *JAMA* No. 8, 281, May 20, 1968; "Referral to a Specialist," 211 *JAMA* No. 11, 1911, March 16, 1970; and "Duty to Refer to Larger Hospital," 224 *JAMA* No. 12, 1687, June 18, 1973.

D. The Texas "Good Samaritan" Law

"No person shall be liable in civil damages who administers emergency care in good faith at the scene of an emergency for acts performed during the emergency unless such acts are willfully or wantonly negligent; provided that nothing herein shall apply to the administering of such care where the same is rendered for remuneration or with the expectation of remuneration" (Tex. Rev. Civ. Stat. Ann., art. 1a [1969]).

Notes

1. Purpose and effect of "Good Samaritan" statutes

"Good Samaritan" statutes have now been enacted in most states (the Texas statute was passed in 1961). The purpose of these statutes is to protect physicians from liability when they stop to render aid at the scene of an accident. The Texas statute, like many others, exempts the physician from liability for ordinary negligence. The risk of liability is limited to cases involving "willful or wanton" negligence. Consequently, physicians may be held liable only if they commit an outrageous act of negligence. For example, a physician under the influence of alcohol who stopped to render aid and significantly aggravated the victim's injuries would probably be outside the statute's protection.

The physician who stops to render aid should remain on the scene until the police and ambulance arrive. In a critical situation, if an ambulance is dispatched without a physician, the physician is probably obligated to accompany the victims to the hospital. However, once the victims reach an emergency room, the physician is not bound to continue treatment. (See Holder, *Medical Malpractice Law*, 9–10 [1975].)

2. Incidence of cases

Because of the threat of malpractice suits, physicians are understandably wary of rendering emergency assistance. This fear may, however, be unfounded. Authoritative studies by the AMA and other investigators have failed to uncover a single case in the entire country where a physician was sued after offering aid at the scene of an accident. (See Holder, *Medical Malpractice Law*, 9 [1975]; Morris and Moritz, *Doctor and Patient and the Law*, 356–357 [1971]; and "This Summer in Samaria," *Emergency Medicine* 161–164, June 1971.)

2.03 PROXIMATE CAUSE

A plaintiff must prove not only that he suffered an injury and that the defendant committed a negligent act, but also that there is a definite causal connection between the two (*Thomas* v. *Beckering*, 391 S.W.2d 771, 775 [Tex. Civ. App. —Tyler 1965]).

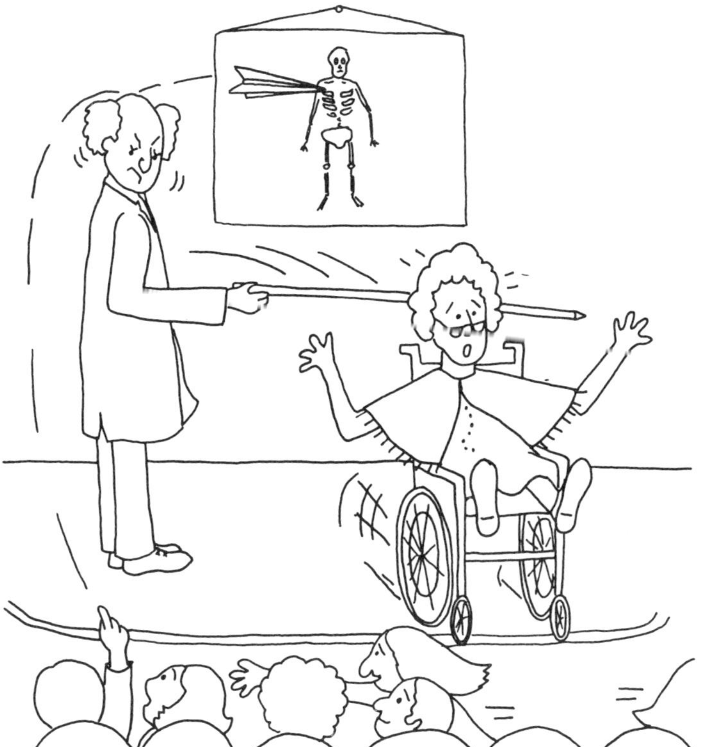

Bender v. *Dingwerth*, 425 F.2d 378 (5th Cir. 1970)

Statement of Facts

1. The defendant-physicians practiced medicine in a clinic in Arlington, Texas. Mr. and Mrs. P were patients of Dr. D, one of the clinic partners. Mr. P was receiving treatment from Dr. D for a diabetic condition which apparently was not disabling.

2. On the evening of January 21, 1966, Mr. P awakened about 11:30 P.M., experiencing sharp pain in his chest and difficulty in breathing. Mrs. P attempted to contact Dr. D but was informed that Dr. E, who apparently had never treated Mr. P before, was on call that evening. After hearing Mrs. P's description of her husband's symptoms, Dr. E advised her that he would meet them in the emergency room of Arlington Memorial Hospital.

3. Mr. and Mrs. P arrived at the hospital twenty minutes later. Dr. E arrived approximately an hour and a half later, having waited at his home until the emergency room nurse notified him that Mr. and Mrs. P had arrived at the hospital. After his arrival, Dr. E examined Mr. P and recorded impressions of early pulmonary congestion. He administered a mild sedative to Mr. P and admitted him to the hospital as a bed patient, prescribing cough syrup. Mr. P had a restless night and died suddenly the next morning of an acute myocardial infarction.

4. Mrs. P brought a suit against Dr. E for malpractice in failing to diagnose her husband's heart disease. At trial, the jury found that, although Dr. E's conduct was negligent, it was not a proximate cause of Mr. P's death. The trial court therefore rendered a verdict for Dr. E.

5. Mrs. P appealed the trial court decision, alleging that the trial court erroneously instructed the jury on the subject of proximate cause. In particular, she objected to the following language:

> And the plaintiff's proof in this respect must not only establish the defendant's act or acts as a proximate cause, but must exclude any hypothesis as to the existence of another efficient proximate cause.

Issue before the Court

Did the trial court's charge to the jury misstate the plaintiff's burden of proof on the issue of proximate cause?

Decision of the Court

The court found the instruction on proximate cause to be "fatally deficient" and ordered a new trial:

> Fairly read, this language instructed the jury that the plaintiff had to prove that Dr. E's negligence was, standing alone, the single cause of the death of Mr. P and that nothing else contributed to that event. In other words, this charge instructed the jury that the plaintiff in order to recover had to prove that Dr. E's negligence was the *sole* proximate cause of Mr. P's death. This is simply not the law in Texas. In a malpractice case, the plaintiff need prove only that the negligent act of the defendant was *a* proximate cause of the injury sustained. . . .
>
> The plaintiff's burden is thus the affirmative one to establish that the doctor's negligence is one proximate cause of the injury. We have not been cited to nor have we found a single case in which the Texas courts have held that the plaintiff has the negative burden of disproving every other possible contributing cause of the injury. . . . The rule, therefore, is one demanding strict proof of causation in fact; it does *not* demand that the doctor's negligence be the *sole* or *only* proximate cause in order for the plaintiff to recover. It merely requires proof that the doctor's act is in fact *a* cause.

The charge in the instant case was plainly prejudicial because it imposed on the plaintiff the burden of proving that the doctor's negligence was the sole proximate cause of her husband's death. (425 F.2d at 380–382)

Levermann v. *Cartall*, 393 S.W.2d 931 (Tex. Civ. App.—San Antonio 1965)

Statement of Facts

1. About 6:30 P.M. on July 19, 1960, Mrs. P's son, Larry, was standing in his highchair (which was twenty-one inches high) when it turned over. He cried violently for fifteen or twenty minutes after the fall and several times during the night. There were bruises on his left hip and left forehead, which remained visible for several days.

2. The next afternoon, Larry vomited after returning home from a birthday party. Mrs. P testified that, after Larry vomited, she telephoned Dr. D, who told her that children fall all the time and that the boy probably had an upset stomach. Larry was very restless that night and, after he vomited again late the following day, Mrs. P took him to see Dr. D. He examined the baby and said all he could find was a sore throat.

3. By Friday, July 22, Larry was weak and could not keep any food in his stomach. Dr. D was telephoned again and he sent suppositories to control the vomiting. On Saturday, July 23, Larry's eyes crossed, with his left eye turning in. Dr. D came by Mrs. P's home on Saturday morning and said that Larry was teething.

4. On Saturday night, July 23, Dr. E, who was Larry's regular physician, returned from out of the city. He was telephoned by Mrs. P and advised of Larry's fall, his drowsiness, vomiting, and the medications given by Dr. D. On Sunday morning Dr. E came to Mrs. P's home and, after examining Larry and again being advised of the history, said that Larry probably had a virus and was dehydrated. Larry was placed in the hospital where he remained until Tuesday, July 26. Dr. E told Mrs. P that Larry's crossed eyes were probably a result of his weakened condition.

5. Larry vomited again on July 27 and Dr. E sent medi-

cine to quiet the child's stomach. Mrs. P telephoned Dr. D again on the twenty-seventh. Dr. D said the history sounded like a deep-seated virus and the treatment prescribed by Dr. E was proper. On July 29, Mrs. P again called Dr. E, who advised continuation of the prescribed medication.

6. Shortly thereafter, Mrs. P compiled a full history of Larry's illness and telephoned Dr. F of Uvalde, who had formerly been their family physician. He recommended that the boy be taken immediately to San Antonio and seen by Dr. G. This was done on Sunday, July 31. Dr. G examined the boy and on August 1 did a bilateral subdural tap and removed 90 cc of fluid. On August 3, Dr. G performed an operation and cleaned out the subdural hematoma, and Larry was dismissed three days later.

7. Several months later, Larry started having trouble with his left eye and was treated by Dr. H, an eye specialist. He performed an operation, but the boy was left with virtually no vision in his left eye.

8. Larry's parents brought a suit against Drs. D and E for negligence in failing to diagnose and treat Larry's subdural hematoma. At the trial, Dr. F testified that the defendants should have recognized from Larry's symptoms that there was intracranial pressure. Dr. H, the eye specialist, testified that "in reasonable medical probability . . . long continued unrelieved intracranial pressure due to the subdural hematoma is what caused the loss of the sight of the eye." Despite this testimony, the trial court rendered a verdict for the physicians and the case was appealed to the Court of Appeals in San Antonio.

Issue before the Court

Did the plaintiff offer sufficient evidence to prove that the delay in diagnosis and treatment was a proximate cause of the damage to the child's eye?

Decision of the Court

The trial court's decision in favor of the physicians was reversed and a new trial was ordered.

The court emphasized the testimony by Dr. H that it was "most probable" that the delay in diagnosis and treatment caused the loss of vision in Larry's left eye. The court concluded:

> The evidence [is sufficient to prove that] the delay in diagnosis and relieving the intracranial pressure was a proximate cause of some damage sustained to Larry's eye. (393 S.W.2d at 935)

Notes

1. The requirement for proximate cause

Bender and *Leverman* illustrate that the plaintiff has the burden of proving not only that the physician was negligent, but also that there is a causal relationship between the negligence and the injuries suffered. No matter how negligent a physician may have been, the plaintiff will lose his case if he is unable to prove (by expert testimony) that negligence was a definite cause of the injury in question.

For example, in *Black* v. *Caruso*, 9 Cal. Rptr. 634 (1961), the victim of an automobile accident suffered severe head injuries. The accident occurred in a small town. Rather than provide any treatment for the patient, the general practitioner who saw the patient ordered him moved to another hospital miles away where a neurologist was available. The patient died in the ambulance and a malpractice suit was brought against the general practitioner. The court found that, although the general practitioner had been negligent in his care of the patient, there was no evidence that proper treatment would have saved him in view of the seriousness of his injuries. The patient thus failed to prove proximate cause and the court rendered a verdict for the physician.

The following notes discuss the leading cases in Texas on proximate cause in medical malpractice cases. (For a more general treatment of the subject, see "Proximate Cause," parts I–III, 218 *JAMA* No. 9, 1479, Nov. 29, 1971; No. 10, 1617, Dec. 6, 1971; No. 11, 1762, Dec. 13, 1971.)

2. The "reasonable probability" test

In *Lenger* v. *Physician's General Hospital, Inc.*, 455 S.W.2d 703 (Tex. 1970), the Texas Supreme Court ruled that proof of proximate cause must show at least a "reasonable probability" that the defendant's negligence caused the plaintiff's injury:

> The proof that must be made to establish causal relation is easily stated in general terms, but it is often difficult to determine whether a sufficient showing has been made to warrant submission of the issue to the jury. Since liability cannot be made to turn upon speculation or conjecture, it is essential that the evidence show at least a *reasonable probability* that plaintiff's complications were caused by defendant's negligence. (445 S.W.2d at 706; emphasis added)

Two years after *Lenger*, the Texas Supreme Court elaborated on the "reasonable probability" test. In *Webb* v. *Jorns*, 488 S.W.2d 407 (Tex. 1972), the plaintiff alleged negligence on the part of a nurse-anesthetist and two surgeons. Mrs. P, a thirty-year-old woman, entered a Fort Worth hospital for the repair of a diaphragmatic hernia. She needed the operation but it was not an emergency situation. Mrs. P died thirteen minutes after the anesthetist began administering an anesthetic. The plaintiff's expert witness testified that in "reasonable medical probability, Mrs. P's cardiac arrest was caused by either an overdose of Halothane or a lack of proper oxygenation."

The court held that this expert testimony satisfied plaintiff's burden of proof on proximate cause because it "eliminated all but two possible causes of Mrs. P's death and both of them were caused by the negligence of the anesthetist" (488 S.W.2d at 411).

3. Requirement for expert testimony

It is worth emphasizing that the plaintiff can prove proximate cause only by offering expert testimony. This is rarely an easy task, as the court in *Bender* observed:

> [T]he plaintiff's expert witnesses are reluctant to state outright that the defendant's act or any other act was a cause of the resulting injury, preferring as medical men to state that such an act *might* have caused the injury. (425 F.2d at 381)

The Texas Supreme Court spoke to this problem in *Insurance Company of North America* v. *Myers*, 411 S.W. 2d 710 (Tex. 1966):

> Reasonable probability . . . is determinable by consideration of the substance of the testimony of the expert witness and does not turn on semantics, or on the use by the witness of any particular term or phrase. (411 S.W.2d at 713)

That decision may have opened the door a little wider for the plaintiff, but the burden of proving proximate cause still remains a major obstacle in most malpractice suits.

4. Misdiagnosis and delay of treatment

In cases where the plaintiff alleges that a physician negligently misdiagnosed his condition, proof of proximate cause requires showing that the subsequent delay of proper diagnosis and treatment actually harmed the patient. In *Levermann, infra*, the plaintiff was able to offer such proof —an expert witness testified that "long continued unrelieved intracranial pressure due to the subdural hematoma is what caused the loss of the sight of the eye."

Compare the case of *Henderson* v. *Mason*, 386 S.W.2d 879 (Tex. Civ. App.—El Paso 1964), where the plaintiff suffered an eye injury in an industrial accident (the facts are fully described in sec. 2.02A). An internist treated the injury with antibiotics and advised the patient to see a specialist if he had any further problems. Two days later, a specialist discovered that a minute piece of steel was lodged in the patient's eye. The steel sliver was successfully removed but the patient subsequently lost all vision in the injured eye and a suit was brought against the internist. The court made the following ruling on the issue of proximate cause.

> It is also clear from the record that [the plaintiff] was never able to prove that any negligence . . . on the part of the defendant was the proximate cause of the

loss of vision in his right eye. . . . [The plaintiff's] own witness, Dr. E, stated that the lapse of time from Saturday night to Monday morning had nothing to do with the loss of vision. . . . Under cross-examination Dr. E stated that, in his opinion, the loss of vision was due to the injury itself, in that [the plaintiff] had a piece of metal propelled into his eye which hit a blood vessel in some back area of the eye, which . . . ruptured causing bleeding into the vitreous . . . [I]t is clear that the evidence . . . fails to prove that, had there been any negligence, such was the proximate cause of "plaintiff's" injuries. (386 S.W.2d at 883–884)

Chapter III

Vicarious Liability

3.00 INTRODUCTION

This chapter is concerned with the legal responsibility of a physician for the negligence of other health care personnel. Under the ancient law of master and servant, a

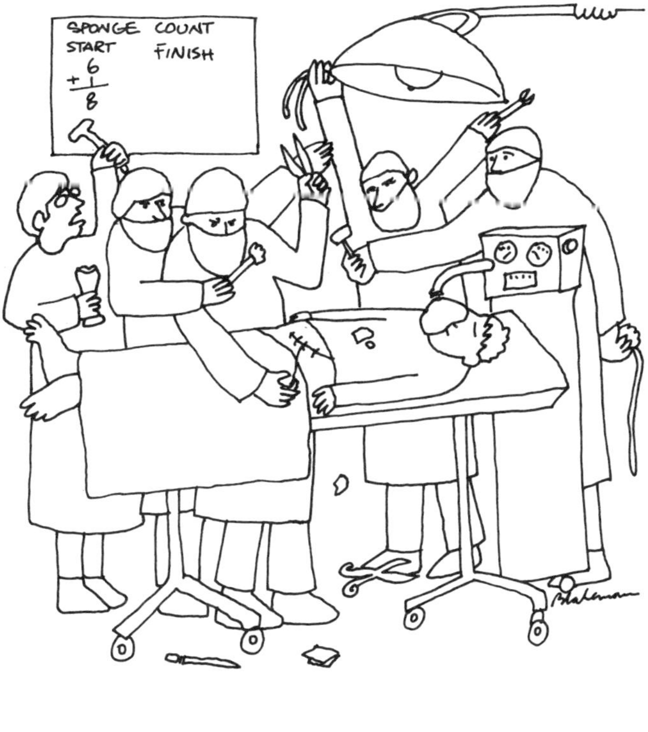

physician may be legally accountable for the negligent acts of other persons even though the physician personally committed no wrong. The legal doctrine governing this situation is known as *respondeat superior*—"let the master answer," or, perhaps more aptly, "look to the man higher up." The courts apply this doctrine to determine whether physicians are "vicariously liable" for the negligence of someone working with them in patient care. Vicarious liability may be imposed even when the physician does not condone the wrongful conduct or participate in it in any way.

The critical inquiry in these cases goes to the nature of the relationship between the physician and the party committing the negligent act. If the court finds that a "master-servant" relationship existed, vicarious liability will be imposed on the physician. The general standard for a master-servant relationship was stated in *McConnell* v. *Williams*, 361 Pa. 355, 65 A.2d 243 (1949):

> In determining whether a person is the servant of another, the essential test is whether he is subject to the latter's control or right of control with regard not only to the work to be done but also to the manner of performing it. . . . The true criterion is the existence of power to control the [individual] at the time of the commission of the negligent act. (65 A.2d at 245)

If the physician is found to bear vicarious liability, the courts will characterize the negligent individual as the physician's employee, agent, servant, or "borrowed servant." The latter term is used when the negligent party is a hospital employee but the court finds that he or she was acting under a physician's supervision or control at the time of the negligent conduct.

3.01 LIABILITY FOR ACTS OF HOSPITAL PERSONNEL

A. Nurses

McKinney v. *Tromly*, 386 S.W.2d 564 (Tex. Civ. App.—Tyler 1964)

Statement of Facts

1. Mark, a nine-year-old, was taken to see Dr. D because he was having difficulty breathing through his nose. Dr. D recommended an operation to remove a nasal obstruction. Mark's parents gave their consent and the operation was scheduled at Methodist Hospital in Dallas.

2. Nurse N, an employee of the hospital, was trained in the administration of anesthetics and assisted Dr. D on several occasions. On the morning of the operation, she mistakenly gave ether to the patient. Dr. D was not present when the anesthetic was administered and was not aware that the patient had been given ether.

3. Shortly after the operation started, Dr. D began to use an electric cautary and an explosion occurred. The boy's lungs were severely burned and he died a few hours later. The child's parents brought a suit against Dr. D for malpractice. The trial court rendered a verdict for Dr. D and the case was appealed to the Court of Appeals in Tyler.

Issue before the Court

Was Dr. D vicariously liable for the negligent conduct of Nurse N?

Decision of the Court

Dr. D was found to be vicariously liable for the nurse's negligence.

This case marked the adoption by Texas courts of the "captain of the ship" doctrine under which a surgeon is generally held to be vicariously liable for the negligence of operating room personnel. The court reasoned that Nurse N should be considered for legal purposes to be an "employee" of Dr. D:

> We have no difficulty in finding that the nurse, although in the general employ of the hospital, was under the facts of this case an employee of Doctor D while in the operating room and under his control. (386 S.W.2d at 565)

The court then applied traditional legal principles which generally hold an employer liable for the negligence of his or her employees. In support of this surgeon-as-employer analysis the court quoted from an opinion of the Supreme Court of Pennsylvania.

> [A surgeon] is in the same complete charge of those who are assisting him as is the captain of a ship over all on board . . . Such supreme control is indeed essential in view of the high degree of protection to which an anesthetized, unconscious patient is entitled. (*McConnell* v. *Williams*, 361 Pa. 355, 65 A.2d 243 [1949])

Notes

1. "Captain of the ship" doctrine

Most states follow the "captain of the ship" doctrine and hold a surgeon to be in complete charge of the operating room and therefore vicariously liable for the negligent acts of surgical assistants. As seen in *McKinney*, Texas (along with other states) applies the doctrine in cases involving negligence by a nurse-anesthetist. (See *Webb* v. *Jorns*, 488 S.W.2d 407 [Tex. 1972]; "Nurse Anesthetists," 211 *JAMA* No. 9, 1591, March 2, 1970.)

It should be noted that two cases involving the "captain of the ship" doctrine are currently pending in the Texas Supreme Court. (See *Worley Hospital, Inc.* v. *Caldwell*, 529 S.W.2d 639 [Tex. Civ. App.—Amarillo 1975]; *Ramone* v. *Mani*, 535 S.W.2d 654 [Tex. Civ. App.—Eastland 1975].) It therefore remains to be seen if the court will move to alter or eliminate the present liability of surgeons for the negligence of operating-room personnel.*

2. Liability for negligent sponge count

In most states, a surgeon will be vicariously liable if an assisting nurse makes an incorrect sponge count and a sponge is left in the patient's body. (See *Harle* v. *Krchnak*, 422 S.W.2d 810 [Tex. Civ. App.—Houston, 1967].) Recently, a Texas appellate court held that a hospital may be jointly liable with the surgeon in such cases (*Worley Hospital, Inc.* v. *Caldwell*, 529 S.W.2d 630 [Tex. Civ. App.—Amarillo 1975]). (See "Hospitals, Surgeons Jointly Liable for Operating Room Negligence," 72 *Texas Medicine* 115, March 1976.)

3. Routine nursing care

In cases involving routine nursing care, the physician is

*See Postscript, p. 109.

generally not liable for the negligence of a hospital nurse unless:

(1) she performs her work under his direct supervision and control; or
(2) he is negligent in permitting her to attend the patient because he knows or should know that she is incompetent; or
(3) in the exercise of ordinary care, he should have been able to prevent the injury and did not do so. (See *Burns* v. *Owens*, 459 S.W.2d 303, 305 [Mo. 1970].)

Thus, the mere fact that a physician gives instructions to a hospital nurse concerning a patient's care does not render the physician liable if the nurse carries out the orders negligently. (See "Physician's Liability for Acts of Hospital Nurses," 209 *JAMA* No. 11, 1791, Sept. 15, 1969.)

4. Nurse's liability

The liability of a nurse for his or her own negligence is treated extensively in 51 American Law Reports Annotated, Second Series, 970.

B. Interns and Residents

McConnell v. *Williams*, 361 Pa. 355, 65 A.2d 243 (1949)

Statement of Facts

1. Mrs. P arranged for Dr. D to deliver her child at the Jewish Hospital in Philadelphia. It was determined that a caesarian delivery would be necessary and the operation was scheduled.

2. Two nurses and an intern assisted in the operation. During the operation, the patient suffered profuse hemorrhages which required "the complete attention" of the obstetrician. After delivery, the infant was turned over to the intern, who was instructed to tie the umbilical cord and apply a solution of silver nitrate to the infant's eyes. (Silver nitrate is an extremely caustic drug requiring careful dosage; proper technique calls for the application of only one or two drops in each eye followed by prompt irrigation.)

3. According to the testimony of one of the nurses, the intern filled a syringe and "squirted" silver nitrate solution once into the child's left eye and twice into the right eye; he then waited "five or ten minutes" before performing the irrigation procedure. As a result of this action, the child's right eye was completely blinded and the left was severely scarred.

4. The parents brought a suit for negligence against Dr. D (the intern was not sued). The trial court held that as a matter of law the physician could not be held liable for the intern's negligence and the case was appealed to the Pennsylvania Supreme Court.

Issue before the Court

Was Dr. D immune from liability because of the fact that the intern was an employee of the hospital?

Decision of the Court

The court found that the physician could be held vicariously liable for the intern's negligence:

> If the defendant had supervisory control and the right to give orders to the intern in regard to the very act (in which) the latter was negligent, it would follow . . . that a jury would be justified in concluding that the temporary relationship between defendant and the intern was that of master and servant, and that consequently defendant was legally liable for the harm caused. . . .
>
> [T]he mere fact that [the intern] was then in the general employ of the hospital would not prevent the jury from finding that he was also at that same time the servant of defendant, if he was then subject to his orders, in respect to the treatment of the child's eyes with the silver nitrate solution. (65 A.2d at 246, 248)

Notes

1. Vicarious liability in nonsurgical setting

The intern's negligence in *McConnell* occurred in an operating room. Under the "captain of the ship" doctrine, such negligence will almost invariably be vicariously borne by the surgeon. In a nonsurgical setting, the legal responsibility of an attending physician for an intern or resident's negligence depends upon the circumstances of the case. Generally, the physician will not be liable if his or her orders involve procedures which the intern or resident may be reasonably expected to perform competently (*Barrette* v. *Hight*, 230 N.E.2d 808 [Mass. 1967], administration of an intravenous solution; *Baidach* v. *Togut*, 190 NYS2d 120 [1959], administration of injection). The general rule was stated in *Stumper* v. *Kimel*, 260 A.2d 526 (N.J. 1970).

> [The attending physician] is not liable for the negligence of a hospital-employed resident physician, when the orders given relate to procedures which . . . fall within the ambit of his training and qualifications, and is the accepted medical standard of practice. (260 A.2d at 528)

2. Negligence committed in presence of physician

The general rule stated in Note 1 applies if the attending physician was absent at the time of the intern or resident's negligent conduct. A different rule is invoked if the attending physician was present and could have prevented the patient's injury. In such cases, the courts generally find the physician to be vicariously liable for the intern or resident's negligence. Thus, when the attending physician is present, he or she is responsible for closely supervising the intern or resident and may bear liability for mistakes which are made. (See "Liability for Resident's Negligence," 213 *JAMA* No. 1, 181, July 6, 1970.)

3. Duty to discover intern or resident negligence

Even if the attending physician is not present at the time of an intern or resident's negligence, he or she may be found liable for unreasonably failing to discover the negligence. In *Moeller* v. *Hauser*, 54 N.W.2d 639 (Minn. 1952), a young boy entered the hospital for a fracture of the femur. Dr. D, the staff physician, advised a resident to use the Bryant's method of overhead traction. This was done and the boy's condition progressed satisfactorily. After about three weeks, another resident examined the boy and determined that the traction had slipped. He took the child out of traction and then reapplied the apparatus. Over the next ten days, a severe pressure sore developed but it was not discovered by the resident. Dr. D did not see the patient during that period and he was later sued for failing to discover the resident's negligence. The Supreme Court of Minnesota held that both Dr. D and the resident were liable for negligence.

4. Personal liability of intern and resident

The preceding notes emphasize that, under certain circumstances, an attending physician may bear vicarious liability for the negligence of an intern or resident. As for the intern and resident, they are, of course, legally responsible for their own negligent conduct and are often jointly sued with the attending physician. (See *Moeller* v. *Hauser, infra*, Note 3.)

5. Hospital liability

The hospital represents a third possible defendant in cases involving intern or resident negligence. Like other employers, hospitals are generally liable for negligent acts committed by their employees and the courts invariably consider interns and residents (along with nurses) to be "employees" of the hospital. (See Holder, *Medical Malpractice Law*, 211 [1975]; "Hospital Liability for Physician Negligence," 214 *JAMA* No. 9, 1755, Nov. 30, 1970.)

3.02 LIABILITY FOR NEGLIGENCE OF OFFICE EMPLOYEES

Rosenblum v. *Bloom*, 492 S.W.2d 321 (Tex. Civ. App.—Houston 1973)

Statement of Facts

1. Mrs. P, a forty-nine-year-old woman, had an appointment with Dr. D, a dermatologist, for treatment of skin blemishes. She was initially examined by Mrs. N, a nurse who had worked for Dr. D only a day and a half.

2. The nurse applied two coats of a 5 percent solution of trichloroacetic acid (TCA) to Mrs. P's face. After the second coat had dried, she took a cotton swab and began to apply 100 percent TCA, whereupon the patient complained, "It's burning." The nurse called Dr. D and he applied various medications to relieve the burning. At the trial it was established that a 100 percent solution of TCA is much too strong to apply to human skin.

3. Scabs formed on the affected area and lasted several weeks. The patient was left with a facial scar and later underwent plastic surgery. Mrs. P brought a suit against Dr. D for negligence and the trial court granted a verdict in her favor. The case was then appealed to the Court of Appeals in Houston.

Issue before the Court

Was Dr. D vicariously liable for the negligence of his office nurse?

Decision of the Court

The court sustained the plaintiff's right of recovery in the case, leaving no question as to a physician's liability for the negligent acts of his employees.

Notes

1. The doctrine of *respondeat superior*

Under the doctrine of *respondeat superior* (let the master answer), physicians are clearly liable for the negligent acts of their office employees. (See Louisell and Williams, *Medical Malpractice*, sec. 16.02 [1973]; "Negligence of Office Assistants," 204 *JAMA* No. 2, 257, April 8, 1968.) As illustrated in *Rosenblum*, the physicians' liability in no way depends upon their participation in the negligent act which injures the patient. It is the mere existence of an employer-employee relationship which leads to the physician's liability.

2. Injections

A number of cases involve the administration of injections by office personnel. If an office assistant injures a patient by negligently giving an injection or injecting the wrong drug, the physician will be vicariously liable. (See "Injections by Office Assistants," 204 *JAMA* No. 4, 193, April 22, 1968; "Administration of Wrong Drugs," 204 *JAMA* No. 11, 225, June 10, 1968.)

3. Delegation of duties

These employee-negligence cases suggest that a physician should exercise great care in assigning medical duties to office assistants. As a general rule, the physician should not delegate functions which require professional judgment as to diagnosis and treatment. (See Louisell and Williams, *Medical Malpractice*, sec. 16.02, 490 [1973]; "Practice of Medicine: Delegation of Duties," 89 *Calif. Med.* 158 [1958]; 1027, "Use of Irregular Paramedical Personnel," 207 *JAMA* No. 5, 1027, Feb. 3, 1969; "Irregular Assistants and Legal Risks," 207 *JAMA* No. 6, 1231, Feb. 10, 1969.)

3.03 LIABILITY FOR ACTS OF ANOTHER PHYSICIAN

Notes

1. Responsibility for negligence of substitute

In a variety of circumstances, a physician may be unable to attend a patient and will arrange for a "substitute physician" to take his or her place. The question then arises whether the referring physician may be held liable for the negligence of the substitute. In *Moore* v. *Lee*, 109 Tex. 391, 211 S.W. 214 (1919), the Supreme Court of Texas ruled that, if the referring physician exercises due care in selecting the substitute, he or she is not vicariously liable for the negligence of the replacement. Most other states follow this principle. (See Holder, *Medical Malpractice Law*, 202 [1975].)

An exception to the general rule applies when the referring physician continues to participate in the case along with the substitute. In this situation, the courts will consider the extent of the referring physician's participation in the case in order to determine whether he or she should bear liability for the substitute's negligence. (See "Liability of Referring Physician," 204 *JAMA* No. 3, 273, April 15, 1968.)

2. Responsibility for negligence of specialist

Most states recognize that a physician has a duty to consult a specialist in certain cases. (See Chapter II, sec. 2.02C.) As a general rule, the referring physician will not be liable for negligence committed by the specialist. This immunity, however, is contingent on the exercise of reasonable care in the selection of the specialist. (See *Ross* v. *Sher*, 483 S.W.2d 297 [Tex. Civ. App.—Houston 1972].) Immunity from liability may also be lost if the referring physician continues to treat the patient along with the specialist. (See "Liability of Referring Physician," 204 *JAMA* No. 3, 274, April 15, 1968; Holder, *Medical Malpractice Law*, 202–204 [1975].)

3. Partnership liability

When two or more physicians create a partnership for the purpose of practicing medicine, each is personally liable not only for his or her own wrongful conduct, but also for that of any of the partners. This principle is generally limited to activities within the "ordinary scope of the partnership business." In the case of a medical partnership, this would mean conduct involved in the practice of medicine. Thus, if one partner is negligent in treating a patient, each of the other partners, as well as the partnership entity itself, will bear liability for that negligence.

In *Kelsey-Sebold Clinic* v. *Maklay*, 466 S.W.2d 716 (Tex. 1971), the Supreme Court of Texas construed the responsibility of a medical partnership to include a duty to exercise "reasonable means" to prevent a partner from using his position to nurture an affair with a married patient:

> [T]he Clinic owed a duty to the families of its patients to exercise ordinary care to prevent a wrongful interference with family relations. It was not required to maintain constant surveillance over personnel on duty or to inquire into and regulate the personal conduct of partners and employees while engaged in their private affairs. But if and when the partnership received information from which it knew or should have known that there might be a need to take action, it was under a duty to use reasonable means at its disposal to prevent any partner or employee from improperly using his position with the Clinic to work a wrongful invasion of legally protected family interests. This duty relates only to conduct of a partner or employee on the premises of the Clinic or while purportedly acting as a representative of the Clinic elsewhere. Failure to exercise ordinary care in discharging that duty would subject the Clinic to liability for damages proximately caused by its negligence. (466 S.W.2d at 720)

Chapter IV

The Requirement for Patient Consent

4.00 THE CAUSE OF ACTION: BATTERY OR INFORMED CONSENT?

The law generally requires the physician to obtain a patient's "consent" before administering any treatment. The legal requirement for consent has generated confusion because it embraces two separate duties. The first, which shall be referred to as the duty to obtain "permissive consent," is based on the law of battery. In the medical context, a battery consists of an unauthorized "touching" of the patient's body. Except in cases of medical emergency, any treatment of surgery performed without the permissive consent of the patient (or guardian) will constitute a battery and subject the physician to liability for any injury or complication resulting from his or her conduct. Under the law of battery, the physician will be liable for such adverse results even if the services were performed without negligence and with the best of intentions.

The second duty requires the physician to "make a reasonable disclosure to a patient of risks that are incident to medical diagnosis and treatment" (*Wilson* v. *Scott*, 412 S.W.2d 297, 301 [Tex. 1967]). In a suit based on lack of informed consent, the patient alleges that the physician negligently failed to discharge his or her duty of disclosure. Thus, the action is a species of negligence—the plaintiff must prove:

(1) he sustained an injury as a result of treatment;

(2) the doctor's duty of care required disclosure of the risk of that injury (sec. 4.01B); and
(3) proximate cause—that, had the patient known of the risk, he would not have consented to treatment (sec. 4.01D). (See *Karp* v. *Cooley*, 493 F.2d 408, 422 [5th Cir. 1974].)

Notice that the patient's claim in no way requires a finding that the physician was negligent in the *performance* of treatment or surgery. Rather, the patient need only prove that some undisclosed risk of which he should have been forewarned resulted in injury.

In summary, battery theory is applied when a doctor performs a medical procedure to which the patient has not given permissive consent. The informed consent doctrine is applied when the physician obtains permissive consent but fails to meet his duty to inform the patient of the risks associated with the procedure.

Moss v. *Rishworth*, 222 S.W. 225 (Tex. Comm'n App. 1920)

Statement of Facts

1. Eleven-year-old Imogene lived with her parents in Center Point, Texas. The parents became concerned that Imogene might need a tonsillectomy and sent her along with her adult sister, Clara, to consult a physician in San Antonio.

2. After arriving in San Antonio, Clara took her sister to see Dr. D. Dr. D examined Imogene and concluded that a tonsillectomy would be necessary. Clara agreed and a date for surgery was set.

3. The operation was performed and the child died while still under the influence of the anesthetic. Shortly thereafter, Imogene's father brought a suit against Dr. D, alleging that, because the surgery was performed without his consent, the physician was liable for battery. The suit made no allegation of negligence.

Issue before the Court

Did the adult sister, as temporary custodian of the child, have the authority to give legal consent to the operation?

Decision of the Court

The court found that Dr. D was liable for battery:

> [A] surgeon is liable for operating upon a patient, unless he obtains the consent of the patient . . . or someone who, under the circumstances, would be legally authorized to give the requisite consent. . . . The physician acted in good faith in assuming the sister had authority to give consent, but the sister was only the temporary custodian of the child, and as

such . . . had no authority to give consent to perform the operation in the absence of an emergency. The parent was the only one who could legally give consent to perform it, and, [therefore], the physician's act in performing it was a legal wrong. (222 S.W. at 225–226)

Luna v. *Nering*, 426 F.2d 95 (5th Cir. 1970)

Statement of Facts

1. The plaintiff, Mr. P, was injured in an industrial accident in which a fragment of metal was flung into his left shoulder. Mr. P was taken to a hospital and signed a printed form of consent to surgical procedures.

2. The defendant, Dr. D, testified that his neurological examination made at that time showed no nerve injury to Mr. P's left hand or fingers. Dr. D ordered bed rest for Mr. P and advised him that the metal particle would be removed the next day. No attempt was made to explain the surgery and its risks to Mr. P. In particular, Dr. D gave no warning that the operation involved the possibility of nerve injury.

3. Immediately after the surgery, Mr. P's left hand was numb and he could not bend his fingers. Later it was determined that a branch of the brachial plexus had been injured during surgery and that scar tissue had formed and was pressing against the nerve bundle. Mr. P brought a suit against Dr. D, alleging, among other things, that the physician had failed to secure informed consent to the surgery.

4. The trial court rendered a verdict in favor of Dr. D and the case was then appealed.

Issue before the Court

Did the fact that Mr. P signed a standard consent form give Dr. D a valid defense to the alleged failure to obtain informed consent?

Decision of the Court

The court found that the consent form signed by Mr. P at the time of his admission to the hospital was "not relevant or material to the issue of informed consent" (426 F.2d at 98). The doctrine of informed consent requires a physician to enlighten a patient as to the risks accompanying proposed treatment or surgery. While such information may be conveyed in a printed consent form, this was not done in the form signed by Mr. P. The general consent form would have protected Dr. D against a charge of battery, but it provided no defense against the suit based on informed consent.

Notes

1. General consent forms

As indicated in *Luna, supra*, a consent form which makes no disclosure of the risks incident to treatment will protect a physician only against liability for failing to obtain permissive consent (battery). It offers no protection against a suit based on informed consent.

Under Texas law, patients who sign a consent form will be deemed to have read the form, even if they claim that they did not do so. In *Drummond* v. *Hodges*, 417 S.W.2d 740 (Tex. Civ. App.—Dallas 1967), a patient signed a consent form for an operation but later sued the surgeon for battery. The patient testified that he did not examine the papers when they were presented for signature. The court held that this testimony failed to establish liability for battery.

In Texas, as in other states, oral consent has the same legal effect as written consent—if it can be proven. If the patient denies that oral consent was given, the issue will be submitted to the jury and the jury may choose to believe the patient. A physician is therefore well advised to obtain consent to treatment in written form whenever possible.

2. Special consent forms

A consent form which does set forth information concerning proposed treatment will be admissible to prove that informed consent was obtained. In the famous case of *Karp* v. *Cooley*, 493 F.2d 408 (5th Cir. 1974), the plaintiff's suit alleged that her husband submitted to a mechanical heart implantation without giving informed consent. The following consent form was offered in evidence:

> *Consent to Operation*
>
> April 23, 1969
>
> I, Haskell Karp, request and authorize Dr. Denton A. Cooley and such other surgeons as he may designate

> to perform upon me, in St. Luke's Episcopal Hospital of Houston, Texas, cardiac surgery for advanced cardiac decompensation and myocardial insufficiency as a result of numerous coronary occlusions. The risk of this surgery has been explained to me. In the event cardiac function cannot be restored by excision of destroyed heart muscle and plastic reconstruction of the ventricle and death seems imminent, I authorize Dr. Cooley and his staff to remove my diseased heart and insert a mechanical cardiac substitute. I understand that this mechanical device will not be permanent and ultimately will require replacement by a heart transplant. I realize that this device has been tested in the laboratory but has not been used to sustain a human being and that no assurance of success can be made. I expect the surgeons to exercise every effort to preserve my life through any of these means. No assurance has been made by anyone as to the results that may be obtained. . . .

In holding that the plaintiff had failed to establish her informed consent claim, the court stressed the value of the comprehensive consent form.

> The consent form is consistent with Dr. Cooley's testimony of what he told Mr. Karp. Although not necessarily conclusive, what Haskell Karp consented to and was told is best evidenced by this document. It is of considerable import that each step of the three-stage operation, objected to due to an alleged lack of informed consent, was specifically set out in the consent document signed by the patient. (493 F.2d at 421)

3. Consent by a minor

As indicated in *Moss, supra*, consent by a minor generally does not give a physician the right to proceed with treatment. *Moss* is considered to be a landmark case because it holds that the physician who treats a minor without proper authorization will be liable to the parents for battery.

There are, however, statutory provisions in Texas (and other states) which give minors the legal capacity to consent to certain types of medical treatment. One statute provides that any person thirteen years of age or older has "the capacity to consent to examination and treatment by a licensed physician for any drug addiction, drug dependency, or any condition directly related to drug use" (Tex. Rev. Civ. Stat. Ann., art. 4447l [Supp. 1974]).

Similarly, another statute empowers a minor to legally consent to medical or surgical treatment if the minor:

> (a) is 16 years of age or older and resides separate and apart from his parents . . . or guardian . . . and is managing his own financial affairs, regardless of the source of income; or
>
> (b) consents to the diagnosis and treatment of any infectious, contagious, or communicable disease which is required by law . . . to be reported . . . to a local health officer (such as venereal disease), or
>
> (c) is unmarried and pregnant, and consents to hospital, medical, or surgical treatment, other than abortion, related to her pregnancy. (Tex. Fam. Code Ann., sec. 35.03 [1973].)

The same statute also states that a physician or medical facility may rely with impunity on "the written statement of the minor containing the grounds on which the minor has capacity to consent to his own medical treatment . . ." (Tex. Fam. Code Ann., sec. 35.03[f] [1973]). (See "Treatment of Minors for Venereal Disease," 71 *Texas Medicine* 96, Dec. 1975.)

More generally, the Texas legislature has provided that, if a minor is in need of medical care and neither parent can be contacted, certain persons can give consent by a written statement conforming to various requirements:

Texas Family Code Section 35.01
Who May Consent

Any of the following persons may consent to medical treatment of a minor when the person having the power to consent as otherwise provided by law cannot be contacted and actual notice to the contrary has not been given by that person:

(1) a grandparent;
(2) an adult brother or sister;
(3) an adult aunt or uncle;
(4) an educational institution in which the minor is enrolled that has received written authorization to consent from the person having the power to consent as otherwise provided by law;
(5) any adult who has care and control of the minor and has written authorization to consent from the person having the power to consent as otherwise provided by law; or
(6) any court having jurisdiction of the child.

Texas Family Code Section 35.02
Consent Form

(a) Consent to medical treatment under Section 35.01 of this code shall be in writing, signed by the person giving consent, and given to the doctor, hospital, or other medical facility that administers the treatment.

(b) The consent must contain:
(1) the name of the minor;
(2) the name of one or both parents, if known, and the name of the managing conservator or guardian of the person, if either has been appointed;
(3) the name of the person giving consent and his relation to the minor child;

(4) a statement of the nature of the medical treatment to be given; and
(5) the date on which the treatment is to begin.

A legal form which satisfies the statutory requirements is given in "Minors Consent to Medical Treatment," 70 *Texas Medicine* 109, March 1974.

4. Marriage and the capacity to consent

Under Texas law, both males and females are considered to be minors until they reach the age of 18 years, unless they are married. If a person under 18 is married, Texas law considers that person to be vested with adult privileges and he or she may therefore legally consent to medical treatment. Although marriages below the age of 16 for males and 14 for females may be nullified, a physician is generally protected if the patient granting the consent is married at the time of treatment. (See "Legislative Changes in Consent for Medical Treatment of Minors," 69 *Texas Medicine* 112, Sept. 1973.)

5. Consent by a spouse

In Texas, a physician who secures permissive consent to treatment from a patient's spouse will not be protected from liability for battery, unless the spouse was formally authorized to give the requisite consent. (See *Gravis* v. *Physicians and Surgeons Hospital*, 427 S.W.2d 310 [Tex. 1968].)

6. Implied consent during medical emergency

In cases of medical emergency, treatment or surgery without the patient's permissive consent will not constitute battery. The Supreme Court of Texas stated this principle in *Gravis* v. *Physicians and Surgeons Hospital*, 427 S.W.2d 310 (Tex. 1968):

We recognize the rule that consent will be implied

> where the patient is unconscious or unable to give express consent and an immediate operation is necessary to preserve life or health. (427 S.W.2d at 311)

The rule applies to both adults and minors. As discussed in Chapter 4, sec. 4.02B, an emergency situation also excuses the physician from the requirement for informed consent.

7. Extension of authorized surgery

As a general rule, a physician may be liable for battery if he or she extends surgery or treatment beyond that which has been expressly authorized by the patient. However, there are some major exceptions to this rule. First of all, if an emergency arises during surgery, the surgeon is deemed to have the implied consent of the patient to deal with the emergency. For example, in *Barnett* v. *Bachrach*, 34 A.2d 626 (D.C. Cir. 1943), a patient was diagnosed as having an ectopic pregnancy. After commencing surgery, the surgeon discovered that his patient had a normal pregnancy but was suffering from acute appendicitis. The surgeon removed the appendix and was sued for performing the appendectomy without the patient's consent. The court held that the emergency situation justified the action taken by the surgeon.

A second exception, recognized in most states, authorizes a surgeon to extend an operation to treat a previously undiscovered problem, if it is medically advisable for the welfare of the patient. In *Kennedy* v. *Parrott*, 90 S.E.2d 754 (N.C. 1956), the court exonerated a surgeon who treated several large ovarian cysts discovered during an appendectomy. The court held:

> [I]t is unreasonable to hold the physician to the exact operation . . . that his preliminary examination indicated was necessary. We know that complete diagnosis of an internal ailment is not effectuated until after the patient is under the influence of the anes-

> thetic and the incision has been made . . . In such case—in the absence of proof to the contrary—the consent will be construed as general in nature and the surgeon may extend the operation to remedy any abnormal or diseased condition in the area of the original incision whenever he, in the exercise of his sound professional judgment, determines that correct surgical procedure dictates and requires such an extension of the operation originally contemplated. This rule applies when the patient is at the time incapable of giving consent . . . (90 S.E.2d at 758–759)

In nonemergency situations, a surgeon is well advised to secure the consent of the patient's family before extending surgery. If this is not possible, the physician should avoid any major extension of the authorized operation, particularly where the patient will suffer permanent ill effects (such as infertility). (See Holder, *Medical Malpractice Law*, 233–235 [1975].)

8. The surgeon's assistant

In Texas, an assistant to the principal surgeon need not obtain special authorization from the patient to participate in the surgery. In *Weiser* v. *Hampton*, 445 S.W.2d 224 (Tex. Civ. App.—Houston 1969), a surgical resident was charged with battery for assisting a surgeon without the permissive consent of the patient. The court rejected the claim and held that consent given to a surgeon must be construed to include consent for him to secure whatever assistance he requires (445 S.W.2d at 230).

4.01 THE DOCTRINE OF INFORMED CONSENT

A. The Patient's Right to Self-Determination

"The root premise [for the doctrine of informed consent] is the concept, fundamental in American jurisprudence, that 'every human being of adult years and sound mind has a right to determine what shall be done with his own body.' True consent to what happens to one's self is the informed exercise of a choice, and that entails an opportunity to evaluate knowledgeably the options available and the risks attendant upon each. The average patient has little or no understanding of the medical arts and ordinarily has only his physician to whom he can look for enlightenment with which to reach an intelligent decision. From these almost axiomatic considerations springs the need, and in turn the requirement, of a reasonable divulgence

by physician to patient to make such a decision possible. . . .

"The context in which the duty of risk-disclosure arises is invariably the occasion for decision as to whether a particular treatment procedure is to be undertaken. To the physician, whose training enables a self-satisfying evaluation, the answer may seem clear, but it is the prerogative of the patient, not the physician, to determine for himself the direction in which his interests seem to lie" (*Canterbury* v. *Spence*, 464 F.2d 772, 780–781 [D.C. Cir. 1972]).

Notes

1. History of informed consent

In the excerpt above, the *Canterbury* court strongly emphasized the right of patients to decide for themselves whether to accept risks associated with treatment. This theme of self-determination pervades the cases and commentaries on informed consent. One of its earliest exponents was Justice Cardoza, writing in the 1914 case of *Schloendorf* v. *Society of New York Hospital*, 211 NY 125, 105 NE 92, 93 (1914):

> Every human being of adult years and sound mind has a right to determine what shall be done with his own body; and a surgeon who performs an operation without his patient's consent commits an assault, for which he is liable in damages.

A more modern expression of the concept appeared in a recent law review comment:

> Since the patient bears the entire risk of non-negligent injury and is concerned with his own interests as no other person can be, it is only fair to allow him to choose between accepting or rejecting the hazards of a proposed treatment even if his choice is irrational . . . Some authorities argue that the average patient

> could not intelligently compare the risks of alternative methods of treatment and the risks of accepting or rejecting treatment. Some authorities insist that the average patient lacks the capacity to make an intelligent choice. However, such capacity is not required by the informed consent theory. The theory of informed consent vindicates the right to decline a risk; it does not insure that the decision is wise. ("Informed Consent in Medical Malpractice," 55 *Calif. L. Rev.* 1396, 1409 [1967])

In the sections which follow, it should become apparent that the doctrine of informed consent has evolved along a path strewn with majority and minority views, qualifications, and obvious ambiguities. If the package seems distressingly untidy, it is well to keep in mind that the courts are struggling to balance a commitment to patient self-determination, on the one hand, and a recognition of the every-day realities of modern medicine, on the other.

B. General Standard for the Duty to Disclose

The legal sufficiency of a physician's disclosure of risks associated with treatment must be judged according to a community standard: "what a reasonable practitioner of the same or similar community under the same or similar circumstances would have disclosed" (*Wilson* v. *Scott*, 412 S.W.2d 299, 302 [Tex. 1967]).

Ross v. *Sher*, 403 S.W.2d 297 (Tex. Civ. App.—Houston 1972)

Statement of Facts

1. In 1933, Mr. P was shot twice during a robbery, with one bullet exiting just below his tailbone. In 1940 he was operated on for a fistula. In 1964, Mr. P saw Dr. D, a general practitioner, who hospitalized him for a rectal abcess. Dr. D determined that the patient suffered from a rectal fistula and referred him to Dr. E, a general surgeon.

2. Dr. E informed Mr. P that a fistulectomy was necessary. He explained that the procedure required removal of all diseased tissue and that "in all probability it would heal well." Dr. E did not, however, advise Mr. P that the operation might result in incontinence. At the trial, the doctor testified that he did not like "the negative approach to surgery" and that, although the fistula was larger than average, his preoperative judgment was that incontinence was only a "remote possibility."

3. Several months after the fistulectomy, Mr. P developed incontinence. He was hospitalized and another operation was performed to correct the incontinence. That operation was not successful and some time later a colostomy was performed.

4. Mr. P brought a suit against Dr. E based on the physician's failure to disclose the risk of incontinence. At the trial, Dr. E and Dr. D testified that the risk of incontinence was too remote to require disclosure. The plaintiff was unable to offer expert medical testimony to contradict this assertion.

5. The trial court rendered a verdict for Dr. E and the case was appealed to the Court of Civil Appeals in Houston.

Issue before the Court

Did the plaintiff's evidence establish a valid claim under the doctrine of informed consent?

Decision of the Court

The Court of Appeals affirmed the trial court's decision in favor of Dr. E.

The court stated that, under Texas law, Mr. P had a "burden to prove by expert medical evidence" that the failure to disclose the risk of incontinence was a violation of local medical custom. Because Mr. P failed to satisfy this burden, the court concluded that the verdict for Dr. E was correct as a matter of law.

Notes

1. The majority rule

Wilson v. *Scott*, 412 S.W.2d 299 (Tex. 1967), is the landmark case in Texas concerning a doctor's duty to disclose risks to a patient. The most significant aspect of the case was the court's adoption of a professional rather than a lay standard for disclosure. In other words, the court rejected the idea that a lay jury should be given complete discretion to decide whether a physician's disclosure was sufficient to avoid liability. Rather, the jury is bound to accept the standard set by the testimony of local medical experts, the so-called community standard. Local medical custom is thus permitted to govern whether a particular hazard should be disclosed to the patient. For example, in *Wilson*, a medical expert testified that a stapedectomy carried a 1 percent risk of a total loss of hearing. He further testified that local physicians customarily disclose that risk. The court held that this testimony established the standard which the jury must apply in evaluating the defendant's conduct.

Texas is only one of a great majority of states applying a professional standard in informed consent cases. The largest group within the majority measures the duty to disclose according to the custom of physicians within the "community." Other majority jurisdictions express the duty in terms of "whatever disclosure a reasonable practitioner would make under the circumstances" or "disclosure consistent with good medical practice." Whatever the formula, these courts all require testimony by medical experts to establish the standard which will be applied to a defendant-physician's conduct. (See "Informed Consent to Therapy," 64 *Nw. U. L. Rev.* 628, 636 [1970].)

2. Application of the majority rule

The significance of the professional standard approach is illustrated in *DiFilippo* v. *Preston*, 173 A.2d 333 (Del.

1961). The plaintiff in that case, a housewife, consulted a surgeon for treatment of an enlarged thyroid. A thyroidectomy was recommended and the woman gave permissive consent to the operation. Although the operation was performed competently, a laryngeal nerve was damaged. The patient was left unable to speak above a hoarse whisper and had to breathe through a tube inserted in her neck. She brought a suit alleging that the surgeon wrongfully failed to warn her of the possibility of these results. At the trial, undisputed expert testimony established that local surgeons did not customarily warn thyroidectomy patients of the risk of injury to the larynx. The same medical experts did, however, concede that such an injury occurred in about 2 percent of all thyroidectomies. Applying the community standard rule, the court held that the surgeon had not breached his duty to disclose.

3. The minority rule

In *DiFilippo, infra*, Note 2, the plaintiff's case was doomed from the outset because local physicians did not customarily disclose that a thyroidectomy carried a risk of injury to the larynx. Under the majority (community) rule, the plaintiff could not even argue that the alleged "custom" was arbitrary or unreasonable—any testimony to that effect would have been excluded as irrelevant to the issues before the court.

Dissatisfaction with cases like *DeFilippo* led several states (California, New Mexico, New York, Oregon, Rhode Island, Wisconsin, and the District of Columbia) to adopt a minority rule which does not allow local medical custom to set an absolute standard for disclosure. In minority jurisdictions, the reasonableness of a physician's disclosure in a given case is left entirely to the discretion of the jury and the plaintiff does not automatically lose if he cannot find a physician to testify in his favor.

As explained in *Canterbury* v. *Spence*, 464 F.2d 772 (D.C. Cir. 1972), the minority rule requires disclosure of all "material" information:

> We do not agree that the patient's cause of action is dependent upon the existence and nonperformance of a relevant professional tradition. There are, in our view, formidable obstacles to acceptance of the notion that the physician's obligation to disclose is either germinated or limited by medical practice. To begin with, the reality of any discernible custom reflecting a professional consensus on communication of option and risk information to patients is open to serious doubt. We sense the danger that what in fact is no custom at all may be taken as an affirmative custom to maintain silence, and that physician-witnesses to the so-called custom may state merely their personal opinions as to what they or others would do under given conditions. . . .
>
> Respect for the patient's right of self-determination on particular therapy demands a standard set by law for physicians rather than one which physicians may or may not impose upon themselves. . . . In our view the patient's right of self-decision shapes the boundaries of the duty to reveal. That right can be effectively exercised only if the patient possesses enough information to enable an intelligent choice. The scope of the physician's communication to the patient, then, must be measured by the patient's need, and that need is the information material to the decision. Thus, the test for determining whether a particular peril must be divulged is its materiality to the patient's decision: all risks potentially affecting the decision must be unmasked. (464 F.2d at 784–787.)

For a thorough analysis of the minority rule, consult "Comment: New Trends in Informed Consent," 54 *Neb. L. Rev.* 66 (1975).

4. Insufficiency of technical language

The duty to obtain informed consent obligates a physician

to communicate medical information in terms which a patient may reasonably be expected to understand. Technical language will not ordinarily suffice to disclose a risk to an untutored layman. (See "Informed Consent to Therapy," 64 *Nw. U. L. Rev.* 628, 643–644 [1970]; "Informed Consent," 214 *JAMA* No. 7, 1383, Nov. 16, 1970.)

For example, in *Gray* v. *Grunnagle*, 423 Pa. 144, 223 A.2d 663 (1966), the court found that the plaintiff had given permissive consent to an exploratory laminectomy without understanding the risks of the procedure. Among other things, the patient did not understand that the term "exploratory" meant the surgeon would "look for and correct if possible." Consequently, when corrective surgery was performed and paralysis resulted, the physician was found liable for failing to obtain the informed consent of his patient. The court held:

> [I]t will be no defense for a surgeon to prove that the patient had given his consent, if the consent was not given with a true understanding of the nature of the operation to be performed. (223 A.2d at 674)

5. Information due without request; waiver

The patient's right to be informed is not contingent on a request for information.

> We discard the thought that the patient should ask for information before the physician is required to disclose. Caveat emptor [let the buyer beware] is not the norm for the consumer of medical services. Duty to disclose is more than a call to speak merely to answer the patient's questions: it is a duty to volunteer, if necessary, the information the patient needs for intelligent decision. The patient may be ignorant, confused, overawed by the physician or frightened by the hospital, or even ashamed to inquire. (*Canterbury* v. *Spence*, 464 F.2d 772, 783 n. 36 [D.C. Cir. 1972].)

The right to information may, however, be waived if

the patient specifically requests that the physician not make a disclosure of risks. (See *Cobbs* v. *Grant*, 8 Cal.3d 229, 245, 502 P.2d 1, 12 [1972]; "The Patient's Right to Know," 17 *U.C.L.A. L. Intra. L. Rev.* 758, 785 [1970].) But the courts may be expected to scrutinize an alleged waiver:

> [W]aiver may be acceptable if courts ensure that the patient is not intimidated into waiving an informed consent by pressure from a hurried physician. If the patient clearly understands that the physician would willingly give the information and that waiver means that the physician will make the final decisions waiver might be permitted, since the patient may determine that the emotional cost to himself of the information or of the decision-making is too great. "Informed Consent and the Dying Patient," 83 *Yale L. J.* n. 126 [1974].)

6. Capacity to grant informed consent

As a general rule, only the patient can grant informed consent to a proposed procedure. Special rules governing treatment of minors are discussed in sec. 4.00, Notes 1 and 2. The advisability of disclosure to the family in cases involving an apprehensive patient is discussed in sec. 4.02A, Note 4.

C. Scope of the Disclosure Requirement

In Texas and a majority of other states, the adequacy of a physician's disclosure in a given case is judged according to the standard of "what a reasonable medical practitioner of the same or similar community would have disclosed." (See sec. 4.01B.) When a case goes to trial, local physicians will be called as witnesses to testify as to whether certain information is customarily disclosed to a patient. The case is required by law to be resolved according to the standard which emerges from such expert testimony. Consequently, the courts which adhere to the "community" rule have not found it necessary to promulgate a set of rules on the *scope* of the disclosure requirement. However, various guidelines have evolved and these will be the subject of the following notes.

Notes

1. General topics for disclosure

First, a summary of topics for disclosure is in order. Two authorities will be quoted—each arguably presents a standard which should be followed by all physicians.

In their treatise on the law of medical malpractice, Professor Louisell and Dr. Williams state:

> Where circumstances permit, the patient should be told (1) the diagnosis, (2) the general nature of the contemplated procedure, (3) the risks involved, (4) the prospects of success, (5) the prognosis if the procedure is not performed, and (6) alternative methods of treatment, if any. (Copyright by Matthew Bender & Company, Inc., and reprinted with permission from *Medical Malpractice* by Louisell and Williams, sec. 22.01, 594, 43–44 [1970].)

The following provisions from the Statement of a Patient's Bill of Rights, drafted in 1972 by the American Hospital Association, offer a more expanded view of the subject:

> (2) The patient has the right to obtain from his physician complete current information concerning his diagnosis, treatment, and prognosis in terms the patient can be reasonably expected to understand. When it is not medically advisable to give such information to the patient, the information should be made available to an appropriate person in his behalf. He has the right to know, by name, the physician responsible for his care.

> (3) The patient has the right to receive from his physician information necessary to give informed consent prior to the start of any procedure and/or treatment. Except in emergencies, such information for informed consent should include but not neces-

sarily be limited to the specific procedure and/or treatment, the medically significant risks involved, and the probable duration of incapacitation. Where medically significant alternatives for care or treatment exist, or when the patient requests information concerning medical alternatives, the patient has the right to such information. . . .

(4) The patient has the right to refuse treatment to the extent permitted by law and to be informed of the consequences of his action. . . .

(9) The patient has the right to be advised if the hospital proposes to engage in or perform human experimentation affecting his care or treatment. The patient has the right to refuse to participate in such research projects.

2. The range of risks to disclose

The most perplexing aspect of the law of informed consent concerns the range of risks which a physician should disclose to a patient. In sec. 4.02, we shall consider the physician's discretionary privilege to withhold information from an unduly apprehensive patient. At this point, however, let us address the problem of disclosure to the patient who can handle a frank discussion of risks.

The courts generally weigh two factors in determining whether a risk should be disclosed: (1) the seriousness of the potential injury and (2) the statistical frequency with which the injury occurs. As one would expect, the courts are most likely to find a duty to disclose in cases where the patient faced a risk of serious injury. (See Louisell and Williams, *Medical Malpractice*, sec. 22.06, 294.54–55 [1970].) Thus, courts have found a duty to disclose the following risks: possible loss of kidney after kidney biopsy (*Miller v. Kennedy*, 11 Wash. App. 272, 522, P.2d 852 [1974]; possible blindness after procedure to remove foreign object from eye (*Garone* v. *Roberts' Technical and*

Trade School, 366 N.Y.S.2d 129 [1975]); high incidence of compression fractures of vertebrae resulting from insulin shock therapy (*Mitchell* v. *Robinson*, 334 S.W.2d 11 [Mo. 1960]); 3 percent risk of death or disability from arteriogram (*Bowers* v. *Talmage*, 159 So.2d 888 [Fla. 1966]); 1 percent risk of paralysis from laminectomy (*Canterbury* v. *Spence*, 464 F.2d 794 [D.C. Cir. 1972]); and 1 percent risk of loss of hearing from stapedectomy (*Wilson* v. *Scott*, 412 S.W.2d 299 [Tex. 1967]).

Conversely, courts have refused to recognize a duty to disclose in cases involving the following risks: .013 percent chance that blood transfusion may cause hepatitis, where the transfusion unexpectedly became necessary during surgery (*Sawyer* v. *Methodist Hospital of Memphis*, 383 *F. Supp.* 563 [Tenn. 1974]); small risk of vesico-vaginal fistula from hysterectomy (*Tatro* v. *Lueken*, 212 Kan. 606, 512 P.2d 529 [1973]); a 1-in-250 chance of perforation of the esophagus during esophagoscopy (*Starnes* v. *Taylor*, 272 N.C. 386, 158 S.E.2d 339 [1968]); 0.5 to 3 percent risk of hypothyroidism following thyroidectomy (*Collins* v. *Itoh*, 503 P.2d 36 [Mont. 1972]); 4 percent risk of minor complications associated with heart catheterization (*Walstad* v. *Univ. of Minn. Hosp.*, 442 F.2d 634 [8th Cir. 1971]); 1 percent risk of testicle impairment following surgery for inguinal hernia (*Rea* v. *Gaulke*, 442 S.W.2d 826 [Tex. Civ. App.—Houston 1969]); remote possibility of incontinence following fistulectomy (*Ross* v. *Sher*, 483 S.W.2d 297 [Tex. Civ. App.—Houston 1972]).

3. Information that need not be disclosed

Disclosure of the following matters has been held to be unnecessary:

(a) Under the "general knowledge" doctrine, a physician is under no obligation to explain to an average patient those matters of which a reasonably informed patient should already be aware. (See "Medical Liability," 1970

Wis. L. Rev. 879, 890.) The doctrine was applied in *Platta* v. *Flatley*, 227 N.W.2d 898 (Wis. 1975), where a doctor was sued for not disclosing that a foot operation might necessitate taking pain medication and might prevent the plaintiff from continuing in her occupation. The court held that the risks fell into the category of "dangers of which persons of average sophistication are aware" and hence did not necessitate a warning from the physician.

Similarly, there is no obligation to explain risks if the patient already has learned of them from another source. (See Louisell and Williams, *Medical Malpractice*, sec. 22.05, n. 22a [Supp. 1974].)

(b) In *Anderson* v. *Hooker*, 420 S.W.2d 235 (Tex. Civ. App.—El Paso 1967), the court ruled that a physician was not required to disclose that a prior patient had suffered a specific adverse result.

(c) In *Bell* v. *Umstattd*, 401 S.W.2d 206 (Tex. Civ. App. Austin 1966), the patient sued an anesthesiologist after suffering an injury to her vocal cords during the insertion of an endotracheal tube. The court held that, barring inquiry, the anesthesiologist was not under a duty to disclose the method he or the surgeon selected for administering the anesthetic. The court stated:

> Surgical operation may consist of many steps and involve many specialists. It would, indeed, be unreasonable and undesirable to place a burden of full and complete disclosure upon each and every specialist involved as to the specific methods intended to be used in an operation and all of the possible risks involved in each step of an operation. (401 S.W.2d at 313)

It is worth noting that in *Bell*, the patient sued the anesthesiologist rather than the surgeon. By implication, the court may be saying that the risk of anesthesia should be explained by the surgeon. (See Perdue, *The Law of Texas Medical Malpractice*, sec. 9.02, 199–200 [1975].)

4. Disclosure of alternatives

When a physician has a choice of more than one method of treatment, he or she has a duty to disclose the alternatives and their respective risks. (See Note 1.) In *Bang* v. *Charles T. Miller Hospital*, 251 Minn. 427, 88 N.W.2d 186 (1958), a patient consulted a physician for treatment of an enlarged prostate. The physician recommended and performed a transurethral prostatic resection without disclosing that the procedure would leave the patient sterile (because severance of the spermatic cords was then "a routine part of the procedure" for a patient the age of the plaintiff). This was a particularly significant omission because an alternative procedure might have been performed, although it carried a serious risk of infection. The Minnesota Supreme Court held that, "where a physician . . . can ascertain in advance of an operation alternative situations and no immediate emergency exists, a patient should be informed of the alternative possibilities and given a chance to decide before the doctor proceeds with the operation" (88 N.W.2d at 190).

5. New or unusual treatment

When a physician plans to administer a new or unusual treatment, he or she is subject to a stricter than normal duty to disclose the risks incident to the treatment and any alternatives which exist. In particular, he or she must alert the patient to the fact that the proposed treatment is novel or unorthodox. (See "Informed Consent," 214 *JAMA* No. 7, 1383–1384, Nov. 16, 1970.)

For example, in *Fiorentino* v. *Wenger*, 280 N.Y.S.2d 373, 227 N.E.2d 296 (1967), a patient underwent an operation to correct scoliosis and died of an exsanguinating hemorrhage. A suit was brought and the court held that the surgeon was liable for failing to disclose that the operation had been performed only thirty-five times, with adverse results in five of those cases.

Informed consent is also a major factor in cases involving outright medical experimentation. Legal problems related to medical experimentation are discussed in Holder, *Medical Malpractice Law*, 249–254 (1975).

6. Drug side effects

When a physician prescribes a drug with a known serious side effect, he or she has a duty to explain the risks involved to his patient. (See *Gravis* v. *Parke Davis & Co.*, 502 S.W.2d 863 [Tex. Civ. App.—Corpus Christi 1973].) However, the physician need not go into technical detail. In *Marsh* v. *Arnold*, 446 S.W.2d 949 (Tex. Civ. App.—Houston 1969), the patient was treated for a serious urinary infection with the drug Kantrex. The patient was informed that the drug could cause loss of hearing and other serious injuries, but was not specifically warned of the risk of damage to the vestibular portion of the eighth cranial nerve. When the patient developed equilibrium problems, he sued the doctor for not fully informing him of the risks associated with Kantrex. At the trial there was testimony that, at the time of treatment, there was no other effective drug to prevent bacterial septicemia and that the patient might have died without the Kantrex. The court held that, under these circumstances, "technical explanations" of possible drug complications were not necessary and ruled in favor of the physician (446 S.W.2d at 952).

7. Physician objections to informed consent

The medical community has hardly extended a warm welcome to the doctrine of informed consent. Physicians allege that most procedures are too complex to permit explanation and that patients generally prefer not to hear the "details." They argue that, the more patients learn about risks and complications, the more likely it is they will refuse essential treatment.

Studies indicate that these objections are based on hearsay rather than actual experience with the effects of full disclosure, and that the physician's own emotional reluctance to confront the patient with stark diagnoses and risks often prevents disclosure. (See "Restructuring Informed Consent," 71 *Yale L. J.* 1533, 1566 [1970].) Investigators have also found that thorough disclosure is the best preparation for successful therapy. The patient who can anticipate pain and discomfort is said to be better able to cope with it when it occurs. The patient's anxiety is diminished, and, instead of engaging in recriminations about the physician's care and skill, he or she can concentrate on the task of getting well. (See Janis, *Psychological Stress*, 368 [1958].)

One recent study investigated the reactions of patients to disclosure of complications which might result from angiographic procedures. Patients were warned of risks ranging from blood clots and hives to paralysis and death. Despite these warnings, 228 of the 232 patients studied gave their consent to angiography and over 80 percent were in favor of receiving such detailed information. The study concluded:

> We believe that we have proven that the majority of patients not only have a right to know but want to know what possible complications may be expected from any given procedure. The concern that informing a patient of possible complications will result in his refusal of the procedure is now outmoded. ("Informed Consent—a Study of Patient Reaction," 216 *JAMA* No. 8, 1325, May 24, 1971)

D. Proximate Cause

When a claim based on the doctrine of informed consent goes to trial, the plaintiff must prove that the physician violated a community standard for disclosure. But the plaintiff cannot stop there. He must also prove proximate cause—that is, he must prove that the failure to inform was a cause of the injuries he sustained. This requires a jury finding that, had the patient known of the undisclosed risk, he would not have agreed to the treatment.

Notes

1. An example of the proximate cause hurdle

The significance of the causality requirement is shown in *McDermott* v. *Manhattan Eye, Ear, Nose and Throat Hospital*, 228 N.Y.S.2d 143, 203 N.E.2d 469 (1964). The case involved a woman with corneal disease in both eyes. She was advised to have surgery but was not warned of the risk of blindness. The surgery resulted in blindness in one eye and the woman brought a suit under the doctrine of informed consent. The court found that the physician had breached his duty of disclosure, but he was nevertheless exonerated. Liability was not imposed, because the court failed to find that the patient would have refused the operation if she had known there was a risk of blindness. Thus, the plaintiff lost her case because she was unable to establish proximate cause.

4.02 EXCEPTIONS TO THE REQUIREMENT FOR INFORMED CONSENT

A. The Apprehensive Patient

A physician's duty to make a complete disclosure of risks is considered to be subordinate to the duty to protect the health of the patient. Therefore, a "therapeutic privilege" to limit disclosure has generally been recognized where a full and frank disclosure might jeopardize the health of the patient. (See *Wilson* v. *Scott*, 412 S.W.2d 299, 301 [Tex. 1967].)

The nature and limits of the privilege were described in *Canterbury* v. *Spence*, 464 F.2d 772 (D.C. Cir. 1972):

> [This] exception obtains when risk-disclosure poses such a threat of detriment to the patient as to become unfeasible or contraindicated from a medical point of view. . . . The critical inquiry is whether the physician responded to a sound medical judgment that communication of the risk information would present a threat to the patient's well-being.
>
> The physician's privilege to withhold information for therapeutic reasons must be carefully circumscribed, however, for otherwise it might devour the disclosure rule itself. The privilege does not accept the paternalistic notion that the physician may remain silent simply because divulgence might prompt the patient to forego therapy the physician feels the patient really needs. That attitude presumes instability or perversity for even the normal patient, and runs counter to the foundation principle that the patient should and ordinarily can make the choice for himself. Nor does the privilege contemplate operation save where the patient's reaction to risk information, as reasonably foreseen by the physician, is menacing. And even in a situation of that kind, disclosure to a close relative with a view to securing consent to the proposed treatment may be the only alternative open to the physician. (464 F.2d at 789)

Notes

1. Emergency treatment without consent

In an emergency situation, a physician is not required to obtain either permissive or informed consent. (See sec. 4.00, Note 6.) When a physician asserts that an emergency situation exempted him from the general requirement for permissive and informed consent, the "reasonableness" of his conduct will be assessed by the jury. (See *Gravis* v. *Physician's and Surgeon's Hospital*, 427 S.W.2d 310 [Tex. 1968]; *Luna* v. *Nering*, 426 F.2d 95 [5th Cir. 1970].) In cases where the alleged emergency presented an *imminent* threat to the patient's "life or health," juries generally conclude that treatment without consent was justified. But in cases where (1) the procedure could have been delayed without serious risk to the patient or (2) the patient voiced objections to the procedure, juries very often find that the physician acted unreasonably and therefore bears liability for proceeding without the consent of the patient. (See "Restructuring Informed Consent," 71 *Yale L. J.* 1533, 1568 n. 103 [1970].)

4.03 GENERAL GUIDELINES

In their treatise on medical malpractice, Louisell and Williams offer the following general guidelines on the doctrine of informed consent. (Copyright by Matthew Bender & Company, Inc., and reprinted with permission from *Medical Malpractice* by Louisell and Williams, sec. 22.09, 594.63–.64 [1970].)

> (1) Unless the patient specifically and explicitly has negated a desire to know about risks, clearly the physician, even without being asked, should state—or by his conduct indicate—something affirmative about them. He should not ignore the problem. He must not succumb to the "doctor knows best" psychology. He must remember that it is the patient's future, not his own, that is primarily involved. He should remember that one of the high arts of medical practice is satisfactory physician-patient communication. How much information he should voluntarily convey, basically is a function of the seriousness of the risks. His affirmative statements should be proportional to such seriousness.
>
> (2) The physician must specifically and fully answer questions about risks put him by the patient. Where the patient truly wants to know, and explicates his desire in questions, the physician must respond with answers that meet the questions. This is the kind of situation where the fullest scope must be accorded the patient's right of self-determination. If that right means anything, it must imply the privilege to seek out specific data as a basis for decision by the patient. The physician cannot evade his responsibility to respond by invoking a mere shibboleth or ritualistic formula such as "It's a serious operation, not done without risk."
>
> (3) On the other hand, some patients do prefer not

to know the details, including the risks, of proposed procedures. Their attitude frankly is: "Doctor, I engaged you because of my confidence in your judgment and skill. I cannot understand all the implications of what you propose to do, and I do not wish to try. Because of my confidence in you, and my own ignorance and fears, I ask you to bear on your shoulders not only the medical burden of procedure, but the moral one of decision." If that is the true attitude of the patient, and he clearly conveys it, there is no reason in law, morals, or public policy why the physician normally should not abide it, if he is willing to do so.

(4) Perhaps above all else, the physician must carefully avoid affirmatively misleading his patient by serious false assurances that there is "no risk," as distinguished from expressions of kindly hopefulness. In many contexts of the human experience, it is the fact of affirmative assurances or conduct that spells out the difference between lawfulness and unlawfulness. Often "affirmative misstatement" is but a synonym for "fraudulent misrepresentation."

(5) In blunt terms, a physician should always refrain from "over-selling" a proposed procedure. The practice of medicine, like life itself, is filled with uncertainties, often tragic ones. As it is the fool who goes about with the constant lyric that all is for the best in this best of all possible worlds, so it is the foolish physician who unduly discounts the harsh realities of the human predicament.

(6) Where a patient himself cannot adequately be warned because of the likelihood of engendering a psychology that may threaten or even undermine the medical procedure itself, it may help nevertheless to explain the risks to another close to him, for example the spouse. Admittedly it is difficult to find a sufficient

juridical basis upon which to justify this advice. One spouse is hardly the natural guardian of the other, in the sense that a parent is the natural guardian of his child.

But to explain the serious risks to a loving wife when the patient-husband is too distraught to bear them, at least helps to negate an assumption that the physician is usurping the function of decision. It helps to place the burden on the person who, in popular understanding and acceptance, is the one most appropriate—conceding the inability of the patient himself—to bear it. It accords with a felt social sense of fitness and justice. In any event there are indications that when "informed consent" is tested by litigation, it helps to show that the physician did the right thing.

Postscript to Section 3.01

On January 12, 1977, the Supreme Court of Texas rendered an important decision on the "captain of the ship" doctrine. Because the type-setting for Chapter III was completed before the case was decided, it was not possible to revise the discussion of that doctrine in section 3.01. Therefore it became necessary to update section 3.01 by means of this postscript.

The reader may recall that the "captain of the ship" doctrine dictates that a surgeon is held to be in complete charge of the operating room and therefore vicariously liable for the negligence of surgical assistants in *all* cases. In *Sparger* v. *Worley Hospital, Inc.*, __S.W.2d__ (Tex. 1977), the Supreme Court of Texas disapproved the doctrine and held that a surgeon bears vicarious liability only when the negligent assistant is a "borrowed servant" subject to the surgeon's "right to control." The court thus overturned earlier cases "insofar as they might suggest that a surgeon's mere presence in the operating room makes him liable for the negligence of other persons."

Exercising traditional judicial restraint, the court did not attempt to fashion guidelines for determining in a given case whether a surgeon's "control" over a negligent subordinate is sufficient to subject him to vicarious liability. Nevertheless, the court's decision is well worth examining.

The plaintiff, Mrs. P, sued Worley Hospital and Dr. D for injuries resulting when a sponge was left in her abdominal cavity after surgery. At the trial, the jury made the following findings: (1) that the nurses on duty during the operation failed to make a correct sponge count and that this negligence was the proximate cause of Mrs. P's injury (the nurses, however, were not sued by the plaintiff); (2) that Dr. D exercised due care during the operation and therefore was not *personally* negligent for failing to discover that a sponge was left in the plaintiff's abdomen; and (3) that "in watching after the sponges [the nurses were not] the borrowed servants of Dr. D" and therefore the surgeon was not *vicariously* liable for their negligence. As a result of these findings, the trial court rendered a verdict against the hospital and dismissed the suit against Dr. D.

The hospital appealed the case to the Court of Civil Appeals in Amarillo and then to the Texas Supreme Court, arguing that the surgeon "must bear the sole liability since the Captain of the Ship Doctrine made the nurses his exclusive employees." As stated above, the Texas Supreme Court ruled that the "captain of the ship" doctrine would no longer be observed in Texas. The court declared that the issue of vicarious liability must now be resolved by examining the character of the relationship between the surgeon and the negligent assistant. If the surgeon has sufficient "control" over the assistant to render the latter a "borrowed servant," then the surgeon shall be vicariously liable for the negligence; if not, the assistant remains the "exclusive employee" of the hospital and the hospital must bear vicarious liability. In either case, the negligent assistant is personally liable, should he or she be sued.

It is important to recognize that a surgical assistant might be considered a surgeon's borrowed servant with respect to certain operating room responsibilities and a hospital employee with respect to other responsibilities. In each case, Texas courts will inquire into the degree of the surgeon's control over the *particular* conduct in question.

In *Sparger*, the court ruled that, insofar as the negligent sponge count was concerned, the nurses were hospital employees rather than the surgeon's borrowed servants:

> We conclude, therefore, as did the trial court, that plaintiff should have judgment against Worley Hospi-

> tal since . . . it was hospital's employees who were negligent. Since the captain of the ship idea is a false issue and . . . the nurses were not the borrowed servants of Dr. D, plaintiff was not entitled to a judgment against Dr. D.

Two factors apparently influenced the court's decision. First, the court pointed out that the defendant-surgeon had no part in the selection of the nurses who assisted him during the operation on Mrs. P:

> [The nurses] were hired by and were the general employees of the hospital and were assigned by the hospital for the operation. Dr. D did not participate in their selection.

Second, and more importantly, the court emphasized that a hospital manual explicitly set forth the procedures which surgical nurses were to follow in making sponge counts:

> The duties of the circulating and scrub nurses were detailed in the hospital's Policy & Procedure Manual. There were general instructions which applied to both nurses. There were specific duties assigned to the circulating nurse and specific duties assigned to the scrub nurse. The procedures for the sponge counts were intended for use regardless of the surgeon who was performing an operation in the Worley Hospital.

Thus, the particular circumstances in *Sparger* led the court to conclude that the surgeon's control over the negligent act was not sufficient to subject him to vicarious liability. In future cases, Texas courts will be called on to perform a similar analysis of the surgeon's "control" over the negligent act in question. As these cases are decided, the boundary between culpability and nonculpability will become more clearly delineated.

Finally, it should be recognized that, wholly aside from the question of control and vicarious liability, a surgeon (like any other physician) has a duty to exercise due care toward his patient. Therefore, whatever his status with respect to vicarious liability, a surgeon will be *directly* liable if a court finds that, in the exercise of due care, he should have discovered his assistant's negligence and minimized the injury to the patient (see Ch. II, section 2.02).

Note on Legal Citations

The "citation" of a judicial decision customarily denotes the following information:

(1) the formal name of the case;
(2) the volume and page of each reporter system in which the case is published;
(3) the specific page, if a particular portion of the judicial opinion is quoted or referred to;
(4) the state or federal court which decided the case; and
(5) the year in which the case was reported.

This information is conveyed by way of a legal shorthand system, as illustrated in the following examples:

(a) *Childs* v. *Weis*, 440 S.W.2d 104 (Tex. Civ. App.—Dallas 1969). The case entitled *Childs* v. *Weis* was decided in 1969 by the Dallas branch of the Texas Court of Civil Appeals. The court's opinion is published in Vol. 440 of the Southwestern Reporter, Second Series, of the West Publishing Company's system, beginning on page 104. If reference were made to a specific portion of the opinion, the appropriate page(s) would be indicated after citing the beginning pages of the opinion—440 S.W.2d 104, 106–107 (Texas Civ. App.—Dallas 1969).

(b) *Wilson* v. *Scott*, 412 S.W.2d 299 (Tex. 1967). The use of "(Tex. 1967)" indicates that the decision was decided by the Texas Supreme Court.

(c) *DeFilippo* v. *Preston*, 173 A.2d 333 (Del. 1961). This case was decided in 1961 by the Delaware Supreme Court. The court's opinion is published in Vol. 173 of the Atlantic Reporter, Second Series, of the West Publishing Company's system, beginning on p. 333.

(d) *Gray* v. *Gunnagle*, 423 Pa. 144, 223 A.2d 663 (1966). This citation indicates that the case was decided by the Pennsylvania Supreme Court. The court's opinion was published in both Vol. 423 of the Pennsylvania State Reporter system and Vol. 223 of the West Publishing Company's Atlantic Reporter, Second Series.

(e) *Karp* v. *Cooley*, 493 F.2d 408 (5th Cir. 1974). The abbreviation "5th Cir." indicates that the case was decided in the U.S. Court of Appeals for the Fifth Circuit (the Fifth Circuit includes Texas and five other southern states). The case is reported in Vol. 493 of the Federal Reporter, Second Series, of the West Publishing Company's system, beginning on p. 408. The U.S. Court of Appeals hears cases which have been appealed from U.S. District Courts (the federal trial court level).

U.S. District Court opinions are published in the Federal Supplement of the West system. Thus, *Dietze* v. *King*, 184 F. Supp. 944 (E.D. Va. 1960) indicates that the case of *Dietze* v. *King* was decided in 1960 by the U.S. District Court for the Eastern District of Virginia and is published in Vol. 184 of the Federal Supplement, beginning on p. 944.

Bibliography

BOOKS

Holder, Angela R. *Medical Malpractice Law.* New York: Wiley-Interscience, 1975.

Janis, Irving L. *Psychological Stress.* New York: Wiley, 1958; reprinted, New York: Academic Press, 1974.

Louisell, David W., and Harold Williams. *Medical Malpractice.* New York: Matthew Bender and Co., 1970.

Morris, R. Crawford, and Alan R. Moritz. *Doctor and Patient and the Law.* 5th rev. ed. St. Louis: C. V. Mosby Co., 1971.

Perdue, J. M. *The Law of Texas Medical Malpractice.* Houston: Houston Law Review, 1975.

Report of the Secretary's Commission on Medical Malpractice. Washington, D.C.: Department of Health, Education, and Welfare, 1973.

ARTICLES

"Abandonment," parts I–IV, 225 *Journal of the American Medical Association* No. 9, 1157, August 27, 1973; No. 10, 1285, September 3, 1973; No. 11, 1429, September 10, 1973; No. 12, 1511, September 17, 1973.

"Abandonment—the Malpractice 'Catch-All,'" 71 *Texas Monthly* No. 4, 118, April 1975.

"Administration of Wrong Drugs," 204 *Journal of the American Medical Association* No. 11, 225, June 10, 1968.

"The Care Required of Medical Practitioners," 12 *Vanderbilt Law Review* 549, 553–556 (1959).

"Comment: New Trends in Informed Consent," 54 *Nebraska Law Review* 66 (1975).

"Creation of the Patient-Physician Relationship," 230 *Journal of the American Medical Association* No. 2, 278, October 14, 1974.

"Duty to Consult Orthopedic Specialist," 204 *Journal of the American Medical Association* No. 7, 249, May 13, 1968.

"Duty to Refer Patient to Medical Specialist," 204 *Journal of the American Medical Association* No. 8, 281, May 20, 1968.

"Duty to Refer to Larger Hospital," 224 *Journal of the American Medical Association* No. 12, 1687, June 18, 1973.

"Guarantee of Medical Results," 219 *Journal of the American Medical Association* No. 3, 431, January 17, 1972.

"Hospital Liability for Physician Negligence," 214 *Journal of the American Medical Association* No. 9, 1755, November 30, 1970.

"Hospitals, Surgeons Jointly Liable for Operating Room Negligence," 72 *Texas Medicine* 115, March 1976.

"Informed Consent," 214 *Journal of the American Medical Association* No. 7, 1383, November 16, 1970.

"Informed Consent and the Dying Patient," 83 *Yale Law Journal* n. 126 (1974).

"Informed Consent—a Study of Patient Reaction," 216 *Journal of the American Medical Association* No. 8 1325, May 24, 1971.

"Informed Consent in Medical Malpractice," 55 *California Law Review* 1396, 1409 (1967).

"Informed Consent to Therapy," 64 *Northwestern University Law Review* 628, 636 (1970).

"Injections by Office Assistants," 204 *Journal of the American Medical Association* No. 4, 193, April 22, 1968.

"Irregular Assistants and Legal Risks," 207 *Journal of the*

American Medical Association No. 6, 1231, February 10, 1969.
"Legislative Changes in Consent for Medical Treatment of Minors," 69 *Texas Medicine* 112, September 1973.
"Liability for Resident's Negligence," 213 *Journal of the American Medical Association* No. 1, 181, July 6, 1970.
"Liability of Referring Physician," 204 *Journal of the American Medical Association* No. 3, 273, April 15, 1968.
"Medical Liability," 1970 *Wisconsin Law Review* 879, 890.
"Misdiagnosis without Fault," parts I–II, 219 *Journal of the American Medical Association* No. 7, 967, February 14, 1972; No. 8, 1127, February 21, 1972.
"Negligence of Office Assistants," 204 *Journal of the American Medical Association* No. 2, 257, April 8, 1968.
"Nurse Anesthetists," 211 *Journal of the American Medical Association* No. 9, 1591, March 2, 1970.
"The Patient's Right to Know," 17 *U.C.L.A. Intramural Law Review* 758, 785 (1970).
"Physician's Liability for Acts of Hospital Nurses," 209 *Journal of the American Medical Association* No. 11, 1791, September 15, 1969.
"Practice of Medicine: Delegation of Duties," 89 *California Medicine* 158 (1958).
"Proximate Cause," parts I–III, 218 *Journal of the American Medical Association* No. 9, 1479, November 29, 1971; No. 10, 1617, December 6, 1971; No. 11, 1762, December 13, 1971.
"Referral to a Specialist," 211 *Journal of the American Medical Association* No. 11, 1911, March 16, 1970.
"Restructuring Informed Consent," 71 *Yale Law Journal* 1533, 1566 (1970).
"The Standard of Care," parts I–III, 225 *Journal of the American Medical Association* No. 6, 671, August 6, 1973; No. 7, 791, August 13, 1973; No. 8, 1027, August 20, 1973.

"This Summer in Samaria," *Emergency Medicine* 161–164, June 1971.
"Treatment of Minors for Venereal Disease," 71 *Texas Medicine* 96, December 1975.
"Use of Irregular Paramedical Personnel," 207 *Journal of the American Medical Association* No. 5, 1027, February 3, 1969.
"Warranties or Guarantees of Results May Create Physician Liability," 72 *Texas Medicine* 89, May 1976.

$9.30